Simple
Sewn Gifts

Stitch 25 Fast and Easy Gifts

Helen Philipps

David and Charles

www.rucraft.co.uk

To dear little Daisy, with all my love.

A DAVID & CHARLES BOOK
Copyright © David & Charles Limited 2010

David & Charles is an F+W Media Inc. company
4700 East Galbraith Road, Cincinnati, OH 45236

First published in the UK and US in 2010

Text and designs copyright © Helen Philipps 2010
Layout and photography copyright © David & Charles 2010

A catalogue record for this book is available from the British Library.

ISBN-13: 978-0-7153-3777-6 paperback
ISBN-10: 0-7153-3777-7 paperback

Printed in China by RR Donnelley
for David & Charles
Brunel House, Newton Abbot, Devon

Publisher Alison Myer
Acquisitions Editor Jennifer Fox-Proverbs
Editor James Brooks
Project Editor and Chart Preparation Lin Clements
Design Manager Sarah Clark
Designer Victoria Marks
Photographers Sian Irvine and Joe Giacomet
Production Controller Kelly Smith

David & Charles publish high quality books on a wide range of subjects.
For more great book ideas visit: **www.rucraft.co.uk**

Contents

Introduction   4

At Home.................. 6

Wake-Up Breakfast Set 8

    Cafetière Cover.............................. 10

    Napkin...................................... 13

    Egg Cosy.................................... 14

Laundry Bag 16

Decorative Bunting............................22

Bistro Wall Hanging 28

Retro Apron 34

Recipe Book 40

Loved Ones 44

Mix 'n' Match Tote 46

Vintage Sewing Set............................52

    Roses Pincushion 54

    Little Rose Scissor Fob...................... 56

    Rosy Needlebook............................ 58

Furry Friend Favourites........................60

    Pet's Toy Bag 62

    For Fido 64

    For Tiddles 65

Bunny Cuddles 66

Dolly's Cosy Quilt.............................72

Get Festive.............. 78

Festive Hearts 80

Christmas Stocking.............................86

Bearing Gifts 94

    Star Gift Bag 96

    Tree Gift Bag 98

    Reindeer Gift Bag 99

    Festive Cake Band...........................102

Mr and Mrs Gingerbread 104

Materials and Techniques....................110

The Stitches 113

The Charts 115

Templates 122

Acknowledgments.............................127

About the Author 127

Suppliers / Index...........................128

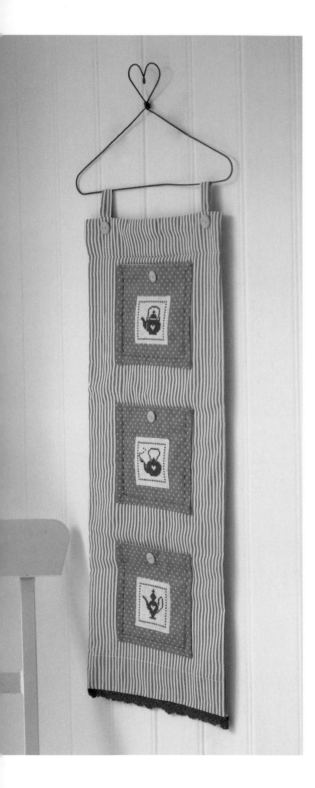

Introduction

Crafting, sewing and home making have enjoyed a huge revival recently and more and more of us are creating things for our homes and families. There is a great satisfaction in producing something from a few simple materials, whether it's a small doll's quilt stitched from scraps or a useful pocket hanger to keep your kitchen tidy. Making a handmade gift is a wonderful way of showing friends and loved ones how much you care.

Many of the projects in this book reflect the comfort and security that home means for children and adults in a hectic, often stressful, world. Making something is a calming experience and there is no doubt that a home is made more comfortable with lovingly created table settings, decorative textiles and special-occasion items. Children learn by watching you sew and can participate as they grow, beginning to stitch simple projects themselves, or finding ways to decorate and customize objects for their own rooms.

The At Home section of this book has a range of delightful projects that will fit into a modern surrounding but also bring a vintage feel. They will allow you to decorate the rooms of your home with sewing projects like a breakfast set, which includes a quilted cafetière cover, felt egg cosies and a linen napkin. There are also items for the bathroom, including seaside bunting and a big striped laundry bag complete with stitched beach hut. A sweet apron and matching recipe book would look stylish in your kitchen and also make great gifts.

There are plenty of treats in the Loved Ones chapter, such as a pretty tote bag, which would be perfect for anyone's mum, and a lovely sewing set of pincushion, needlebook and scissor fob. Two utterly charming gifts for children, a sweet rabbit toy and a colourful doll's quilt, will have you reaching eagerly for your needle and thread. Even the family pets are not forgotten, with useful pet toy bags and fun toys for dogs and cats.

The Get Festive section has something for everyone to reflect the homely joys of the festive season, whether it's decorating the house or giving hand-sewn gifts. There is a shaped gingerbread man and woman toy, a beautiful patchwork, appliquéd and embroidered Christmas stocking, table decoration gift bags and delicious tree heart decorations in fresh, contemporary fabrics.

This collection has something for everyone, so take some time to create something simple but charming and you will feel relaxed and content as your projects take shape and life becomes sweeter.

At Home

Wake-Up Breakfast Set

This colourful breakfast set means you can have flowers on the table every day of the year. The cafetière cover is so easy to make, and very pretty with its bright cotton print. The sweet egg cosies are made from felt with printed cotton linings, and you can make them to match or create a different coloured one for each family member. The linen napkin is quick to make but adds a special touch.

perfect for ...

• adding home style and fun to the breakfast table

• lovers of coffee who like it hot

• quick gifts for someone moving into a new home

You Will Need

- Scrap of white 14-count Aida

- DMC stranded cottons as in chart key

- Tapestry needle size 24–26

- Scrap of green felt for four leaves

- Fusible web (such as Bondaweb)

- Pinking shears to cut out the patch

- Two pieces of printed cotton each 34 x 17.8cm (13½ x 7in) plus seam allowance

- Cotton wadding (batting) 33 x 16cm (13 x 6¼in)

- Two buttons

- Matching sewing cotton

- Selvedges or narrow strips cut from cotton fabrics for six ties

- Stranded cotton to match colour of ties

Finished size: 34 x 17.8cm (13½ x 7in)

Cafetière Cover

This cafetière cover will not only keep your coffee hot but bring a splash of colour to your breakfast table. The cover is very easy to sew – measure the height and circumference of your own cafetière to check how much printed cotton you need.

Sewing the motif

Stitch the motif from the centre of the Aida and centre of the flower motif of your choice from the chart on page 115, using two strands of stranded cotton over one block of Aida. If you are using a button for the flower centre, iron the fusible web on the back of the motif and then sew on the button with matching thread. Cut out a patch using pinking shears five blocks away from the stitching.

Sewing the cover

1 To sew the ties, take a strip of selvedge and turn in the cut edge to the centre, then turn the edge over it and secure in place with running stitches using matching stranded cotton. Press the tie. Make five more to match, or from different strips.

2 To sew the cover, first measure your cafetière circumference and height and then add 2cm (¾in) for seams all round. Lay out your printed fabric and mark the measurements, making a small curve in the centre top to accommodate the spout (a).

3 Cut out two pieces for the back and front, and cut out a piece of wadding (batting) slightly smaller. Place right sides together and pin the ties in position along the side edges.

4 Machine round the two pieces of printed cotton, catching the ties in the seams and leaving a gap for turning in the bottom seam. Turn right side out and press.

5 Place the wadding inside the cover and pin. Sew up the gap in the seam. Using thread to match the fabric, quilt round the outside of the cover and sew several vertical lines of quilting to secure the wadding in place (b).

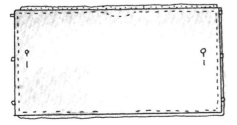

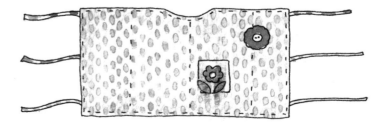

Decorating the cover

1 Fuse your embroidered flower patch on to the cafetière cover in a position of your choice. See page 111 for using fusible web. Sew or glue on two leaves cut from felt.

2 Make a yo-yo from a scrap of printed cotton (see page 112 for instructions) and sew on to the cover with a button in the centre. Sew on two green felt leaves, tucking them in behind the yo-yo.

Unique embellishments make a big statement on everyday items.

You Will Need

- 28-count evenweave in pastel pink 35.5cm (14in) square

- DMC stranded cottons as in chart key

- Tapestry needle size 24–26

- Matching sewing thread

- Two small pastel buttons

Finished size: 33 x 33cm (13 x 13in)

Napkin

This linen napkin takes hardly any time to make but adds a special touch to the breakfast table. Why not make one for each family member?

Sewing the motif

1 Hem the four sides of the evenweave square by hand or sewing machine using matching sewing thread **(a)**.

2 Cross stitch the motif from the chart on page 115, using two strands of stranded cotton over two threads of evenweave. Stitch the motif in one corner of the evenweave square, about 7.5cm (3in) from the edges.

Decorating the napkin

1 Using matching stranded cotton, sew a button in the centre of the cross stitch motif.

2 Make a yo-yo with a button in the centre (see instructions on page 112). Using two strands of green stranded cotton sew a line of cross stitches to form a small corner border from the centre of the yo-yo.

You Will Need

(for one cosy)

- Scrap of white 14-count Aida

- DMC stranded cottons as in chart key

- Tapestry needle size 24–26

- Two pieces of coloured felt, each
  12 x 10.8cm (4¾ x 4¼in)

- Two pieces of printed cotton for lining,
  each 15cm (6in) square

- Pastel buttons, one small and two medium

- Fusible web (such as Bondaweb)

- Pinking shears to cut out the patch

Finished size: 12 x 10.8cm (4¾ x 4¼in)

perfect for ...

- those who love to make the first
  meal of the day extra special
- extra birthday gifts for children
- using up scraps of fabrics

Egg Cosy

These three egg cosies are so sweet and colourful
that everyone in the family is sure to want one.
They are made from felt with printed cotton
linings, with yo-yo embellishments adding a fun
finishing touch.

Sewing the motif

Stitch the motif from the centre of the Aida and centre of the chart on page 115, using two strands of stranded cotton over one block of Aida. Iron the fusible web onto the back of the motif. Cut out a patch using pinking shears three holes away from the stitching.

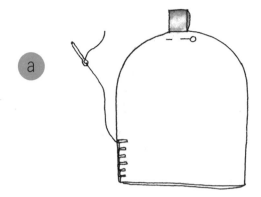

Sewing the cosy

1 Using the template on page 122, draw the egg cosy shape on the felt and cut out. Using coloured embroidery thread, sew round the outside of the egg cosy shape **(a)** with blanket stitch (see page 113).

2 Use the same template to cut out the lining from printed cotton, but add 6mm (¼in) seam allowances all round for these. With right sides together, machine around the lining and then trim the seams **(b)**.

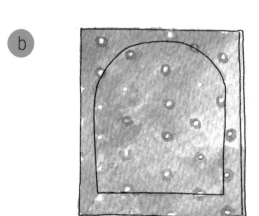

3 Place the lining in the egg cosy and make sure it is pushed right to the top neatly. Turn the bottom of the egg cosy up so the lining makes a border and slip stitch in place.

Decorating the cosy

1 Take the cross stitch patch, place it right side up on the cosy and use a medium-hot iron to fuse the patch to the cosy.

2 Make a yo-yo from printed cotton (see instructions on page 112) and sew on to the corner of the patch. Using matching thread, sew on the three buttons to finish **(c)**.

Laundry Bag

This laundry bag with its jaunty beach hut patch is perfect for a seaside-inspired bathroom. It's a useful family size with a chunky rope drawstring and is really easy to make. The chunky freehand stitches around the appliqué patch add to the rustic charm of this project. You could also add a button or two to the patch – check your button box or local vintage fair for the perfect ones.

perfect for ...

• tidying and storing children's toys
• taking play equipment to the beach for a fun day out
• sewing the embroidered patch to a T-shirt or sun hat

You Will Need

- 28-count linen in cream 12 x 9cm
  (4¾ x 3½in)

- DMC stranded cottons as in chart key

- Tapestry needle size 24–26

- Two pieces of striped ticking in soft red and
  cream, each 66 x 40cm (26 x 15½in), plus
  seam allowances

- White cotton for lining the patch 12 x 9cm
  (4¾ x 3½in)

- Matching sewing thread

- Cream cotton cord 1.7m (2yd)

- Fusible web (such as Bondaweb)

Finished size: 66 x 40cm (26 x 15½in)

Sewing the motif

Stitch the motif from the centre of the linen and
the centre of the chart on page 116. Stitch over
two threads of linen, using two strands of stranded
cotton for the cross stitches and one strand for the
backstitches. Iron fusible web on the back of the motif.

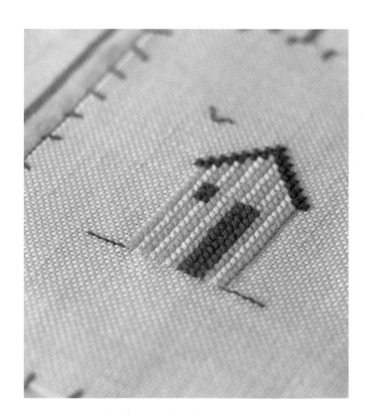

Sewing the bag

1 From the ticking fabric cut out one front and one back piece for the bag, each 68.5 x 42cm (27 x 16½in), which includes 1.3cm (½in) seam allowances (a). Make a hem on the wrong side of the pieces at the top. Fold over the hemmed edge to the right side so it is 9.5cm (3¾in) deep (b).

2 Machine stitch two rows for two casings across the tops of the pieces – these will become channels for the drawstring (c). Place the fabric pieces right sides together and stitch round the two sides and the bottom (d). Turn the bag through to the right side and press the seams.

3 Take the cotton cord and cut it into two equal lengths. Thread the cord through the two casings, one length facing left and the other facing right. Tie the ends of the cord together in a knot.

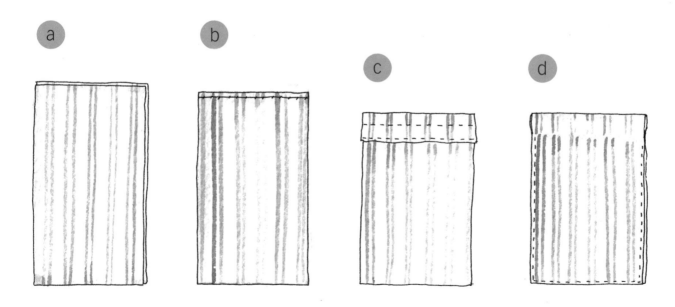

a

b

c

d

Decorating the bag

1 Iron the piece of plain white cotton fabric to the back of the embroidered piece to fuse them together. Iron fusible web on to the back of the white cotton. Trim the patch to 12 x 9cm (4¾in x 3½in) and then fuse the patch to the laundry bag **(e)**.

2 Using two strands of red stranded cotton sew large decorative stitches randomly around the edges of the patch.

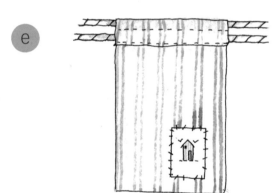

Need another quick gift?

- Make a second laundry bag in a darker fabric, so you'll have one for your 'whites' and one for 'colours'.
- Wish someone a great holiday by stitching the cross stitch beach hut and mounting it in a greetings card.

Laundry Bag

This useful laundry bag will bring a fresh, nautical feel to your bathroom.

Decorative Bunting

This pretty bunting makes a delightful decoration for a bathroom. It is made from triangles of soft shades of linen, delicately stitched with pastel-coloured boats and beach huts. Little buttons decorate the string between each triangle. You could also sew little mother-of-pearl buttons below the cross stitch motifs near the point of each triangle, or search out seaside-themed buttons.

perfect for ...

- a fun decoration in a child's room
- edging a table for a summer barbeque
- decorating a getaway cottage

You will need

(for a six-flag length)

- 28-count linen six 19cm (7½in) squares
  – two in pale blue, two in pale pink and two
  in white or cream

- DMC stranded cottons as in chart key

- Tapestry needle size 24–26

- Washable or erasable pen

- Fusible web in a narrow width (such
  as Wonderweb)

- Bias binding in turquoise 1.3cm (½in) wide
  x 2.75m (3yd) approx

- Pinking shears

- Anti-fray liquid (such as Fray Check)

- Five small pastel buttons

Finished size: 18 x 104cm (7 x 41in)

for six flags (excluding ties)

Preparing the flags

1 Using the template provided on page 125 draw the
triangles on to the coloured linen squares using an
erasable pen. You can make the bunting longer by cutting
more linen squares to create more flags.

2 Sew along the pen line **(a)** and then cut out 2cm (¾in)
away from the stitching all round using pinking shears.
To reduce fraying along the pinked edge apply a liquid such
as Fray Check. Turn over the top of the triangle (the widest
part) and use a strip of fusible web to seal the seam.

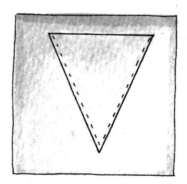

Decorative Bunting

Sewing the motifs

Use the cross stitch charts on page 116 for the beach huts and boats and stitch the motifs in the centre of the linen triangles working over two threads of linen. Use two strands of stranded cotton for the cross stitches and one strand for the backstitches (b).

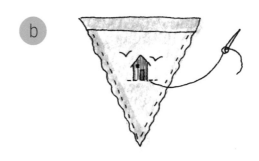

Making up the bunting

1 When you have finished the stitching on the triangles, pin the bias binding in place along the top of the triangles, allowing long tails of binding at either end for tying up the binding. Tack (baste) the binding in position and then stitch two rows of decorative running stitch all along the binding using two strands of DMC cotton in white **(c)**.

2 Finally, add an extra decorative touch by using matching thread to sew on small buttons where the triangles meet at the top of the binding.

Need another quick gift?

- Stitch the motifs and make them up as little framed pictures.

- Use the sail boat motifs to decorate children's summer clothing.

This bunting is so simple and yet will bring a feel-good celebration look wherever it is used.

Bistro Wall Hanging

This colourful wall hanging is both useful and pretty – surely the perfect present. Its three lovely big pockets will store your recipe cuttings, notes, pens, string and other bits and bobs. Each pocket is decorated with a pretty patch showing a cross stitched motif of a vintage-style coffee pot, teapot and kettle – so why not reward yourself with a cuppa when you've finished?

perfect for ...

• coffee and tea lovers
• organizational divas
• adding individuality to a new home

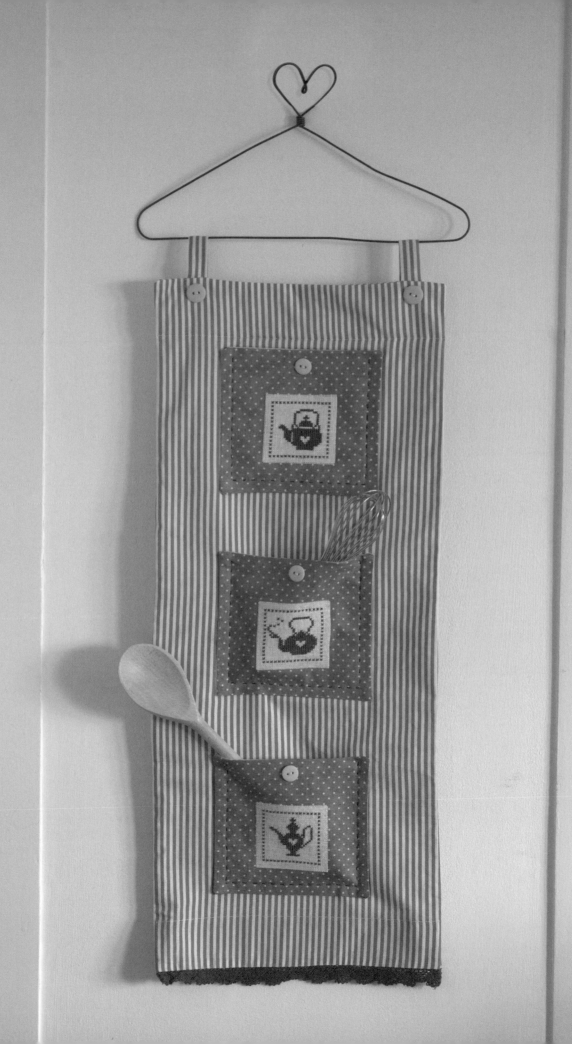

You Will Need

- White 28-count linen, three 9cm (3½in) squares

- DMC stranded cotton in dark pink (DMC 601)

- Tapestry needle size 24–26

- Fusible web (such as Bondaweb)

- Pink and white striped cotton fabric, two pieces each 65 x 28cm (25½ x 11in) for the hanging and two pieces 15 x 1.3cm (6 x ½in) for loops

- Pink and white spotted fabric, three pieces for pockets each 16.5 x 15cm (6½ x 6in)

- Pink and white gingham fabric, three pieces for pocket linings each 16.5 x 15cm (6½ x 6in)

- Wadding (batting) 65 x 28cm (25½ x 11in)

- Deep pink cotton lace 5cm (¾in) wide x 26.7cm (10½in) long

- Five decorative buttons: two large, three small

- Two popper fasteners

- Heart metal hanger (Debbie Cripps – see Suppliers)

Finished size: 63.5 x 26.7cm (25 x 10½in) excluding hanging loops

Sewing the motifs

Find the centres of the squares of white 28-count linen and using the chart on page 117 cross stitch the motifs, using two strands of stranded cotton and working over two threads of fabric. When all the stitching is complete iron fusible web on to the back of each square. Cut out carefully leaving a small border all the way around the stitching.

Making the hanging

1 Take the two 65 x 28cm (25½ x 11in) pieces of pink striped cotton and sew a length of pink cotton lace to one piece at the shorter end – this will be the bottom of the hanging (a).

2 Make two hanging loops using two strips of cotton 15 x 1.3cm (6 x ½in). For each loop, sew up one side and turn out (b). Press in half with the seam up the centre back. Use 6mm (¼in) seams throughout.

3 Place the front and back pieces of the hanging together with the loops in between at the top of the hanging, about 3.8cm (1½in) in from each edge. Sew round the hanging on three sides, leaving the bottom unstitched. Turn right side out and press.

4 Place a piece of wadding inside the hanging, trimmed to size, hidden behind the lace decoration. Slipstitch the bottom closed.

5 For the pockets, use the three 16.5 x 15cm (6½ x 6in) pieces of pink and white cotton fabric and three matching pieces of pink and white gingham fabric for the linings. With right sides together sew the pocket fronts and linings together, leaving a small gap at the bottom of each for turning through (c). Clip the corners and turn out, making sure the corners are sharp. Sew up the gap and then press the pockets (d).

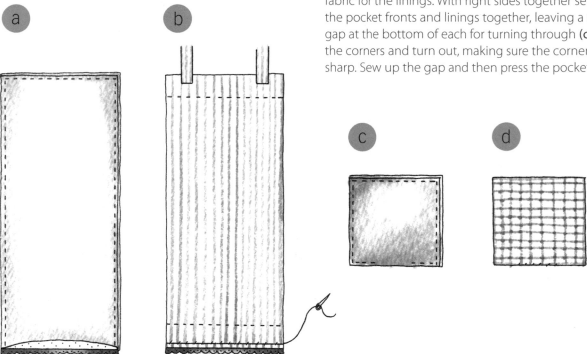

6 Pin the pockets to the hanging with a gap of about 5cm (2in) between each one. Top stitch each pocket in place using two strands of red stranded cotton (e). Fuse the cross stitch motifs in place on the pocket fronts.

7 Sew a button on each pocket and two buttons on the front of the wall hanging. Sew poppers on the back of the hanging to close the loops easily. To finish, attach the hanging to the metal heart hanger – and put the kettle on!

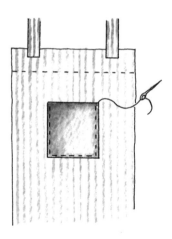

Need another quick gift?

- Make a cross-stitched pocket and use it to adorn a ready-made café apron – instant Parisienne style!

- Stitch and frame the motifs as little pictures.

- For a quick, practical and thrifty gift, use scraps of patterned fabric instead of cross stitch for the pockets.

Make this wall hanging in the cheerful candy stripe shown here or change the colours and hanger to match your home.

Retro Apron

This pretty, hostess-style apron is so easy to make that you'll want one for every day of the week – it's perfect to give as a gift too. An adorable little pocket is adorned with a stitched birdhouse patch and you can add any little buttons of your choice to embellish it further. You could easily make another apron in thicker fabric and with a bigger pocket for light gardening work.

perfect for ...

- those who love to cook
- busy mums juggling home and work
- using the design for a spring birthday card

You will need

- Two pieces of 28-count linen in cream for pocket, each 13.5 x 12.5cm (5¼ x 5in)

- DMC stranded cottons as in chart key

- Tapestry needle size 24–26

- Blue print cotton fabric: 66 x 68cm (26 x 26¾in) for skirt; 11 x 43cm (4¼ x 17in) for waistband and two strips 11 x 102cm (4¼ x 40in) each for ties (add seam allowances to all pieces)

- Ric-rac braid in blue 36cm (14in) long

- Tiny flower and coloured buttons (Just Another Button Company – see Suppliers)

- Sewing thread in cream and blue

Finished size: 66cm (26in) long, with 43cm (17in) waistband, excluding ties

Sewing the motif

Take one piece of the cream linen and stitch the birdhouse motif in the centre using the chart on page 117. Stitch over two threads of linen, using two strands of stranded cotton for the cross stitches and one strand for the backstitches **(a)**. Sew on the decorative buttons, as shown in the photograph. If you do not wish to use buttons, stitch the flowers from the chart instead.

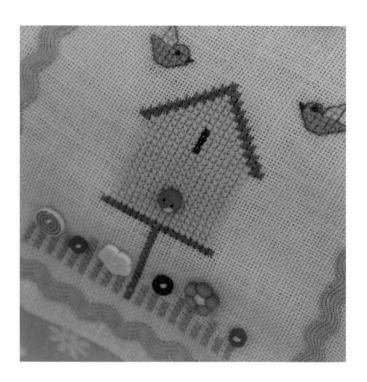

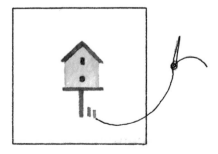

a

Retro Apron

Sewing the apron

1 Take the fabric piece for the apron skirt and sew a hem around the bottom and two sides. Sew a running stitch along the top and draw up gently to gather the fabric (b).

2 Take the waistband fabric strip, fold it in half lengthways and press (c).

3 Pin the right side of the waistband seam to the front of the apron and stitch in place (d). Fold the waist band over to the back and slipstitch in place.

4 With the ties right sides together, sew along the outer edge of the ties. Turn through to the right side and press. Insert the ties into the open ends of the waistband and sew in place (e).

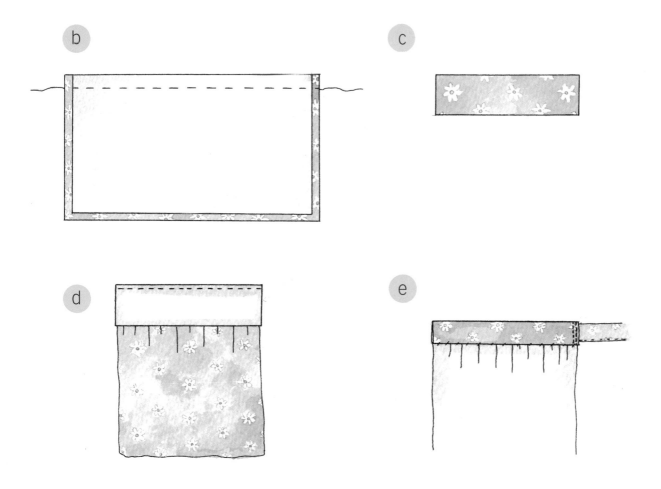

b

c

d

e

Sewing the pocket

1 Take the second piece of cream linen and place it right sides together with the embroidered piece (**f**). Sew round the four sides, leaving a small gap for turning (**g**). Trim the seams and clip the comers. Turn right side out and press carefully, avoiding the buttons.

2 Pin the pocket on to the front of the apron and stitch in place round the two sides and the base of the pocket using matching thread. To finish, decorate the pocket by stitching on the ric-rac braid.

 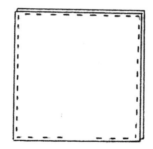

Need another quick gift?

- Create a garden-themed apron with two useful pockets for a green-fingered friend.

- Stitch the design and mount it into a greetings card.

- Sew the embroidered patch to a little ready-made tote bag.

Retro Apron

This darling apron is so easy to make and so useful that you'll want all your friends to have one.

Recipe Book

This charming combination of simple cross stitch and easy papercrafts makes a wonderful adornment for a book – ideal for your favourite recipes. The decorative sleeve on the book slides on and off, so it can be replaced if need be. You can decorate the book with chipboard flowers as shown here, or use buttons to match the apron and give both as a special gift, perhaps with a matching cross stitch tag.

perfect for ...

- inventive cooks to keep all their recipes
- fanatical note-takers and list-makers
- bird watchers who love to record their sightings

You will need

- 14-count Aida in cream 10cm (4in) square

- DMC stranded cottons as in chart key

- Tapestry needle size 24–26

- Patterned hardback notebook A5 size

- Contrast patterned paper

- Thin white card and red card

- Three chipboard flowers

- Double-sided adhesive tape

Finished size: 21 x 15cm (8¼ x 6in)

Sewing the motif

Following the chart on page 117, stitch the smaller birdhouse with the bird on top. Stitch over one block of Aida, using two strands of stranded cotton for the cross stitches and one strand for the backstitches. When the stitching is complete, cut out the motif two blocks away from the stitching all the way round and use double-sided tape to fix a piece of white card on the back of the embroidery.

Making the sleeve

1 Cut a piece of red card slightly bigger than the embroidery and fix the embroidery to the card using double-sided tape.

2 Cut a piece of patterned paper 7cm (2¾in) wide x the depth of your notebook plus 10cm (4in) extra to fold inside the book. Fold the paper around the front cover of the book and then use double-sided tape to attach a smaller strip 15 x 3.5cm (6 x 1½in) to the two folded-in ends (a). This means the paper can be slipped on and off easily.

3 Attach the mounted cross stitch to the front of the patterned paper strip with double-sided tape (b). Decorate with chipboard flowers to finish.

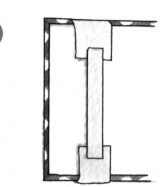

a

b

Need another quick gift?

- Make a simple mobile phone cover and sew the embroidered patch to it.
- For a more durable book cover sew the patch to a fabric cover.

Loved Ones

Mix 'n' Match Tote

Making a unique tote bag for a special person is a great way to say thank you for all the things they do for you. This pretty design mixes fabrics and is a breeze to make. It's decorated with appliquéd borders – one cut from a printed floral fabric, the other cross stitched on linen for a tactile contrasting texture. The same floral motif decorates the handmade fabric buttons that look so cute on the handles.

perfect for …

• anyone who just adores bags!
• busy girls of any age
• fabric lovers

You Will Need

- Pewter 28-count linen 31.5 x 6cm (12 x 2½in) and four scraps for buttons

- DMC stranded cotton in pale pink

- Tapestry needle size 24–26

- Grey and pink floral fabric for bag 18 x 33cm (7 x 13in)

- Grey and white spot fabric for bag, one piece for bag front 18 x 33cm (7 x 13in) and one for bag back 40.5 x 33cm (16 x 13in)

- Grey and white spot fabric for handles, two strips 3.8 x 78cm (1½ x 30in)

- Rose print stripe fabric for bag 5 x 33cm (2 x 13in)

- White and grey spot fabric for lining, two pieces 39.5 x 32cm (15½ x 12½in)

- Small amount of polyester filling for buttons

Finished size: 38 x 30.5cm (15 x 12in) excluding handles

Sewing the motif

Take the strip of 28-count pewter linen and fold it in quarter to find the centre and begin stitching. Use the chart on page 118 to cross stitch the flowers over two threads of linen, using two strands of stranded cotton.

Sewing the bag

1 For the bag front, take the piece of grey and pink floral fabric and the 18 x 33cm (7 x 13in) piece of grey and white spot fabric and join the two fabrics with a 6mm (¼in) seam to create the bag front (a).

2 Press a hem around all sides of the cross stitched linen border and appliqué it to the front of the bag over the central join. Use deep pink cotton to make cross stitches at 2cm (¾in) intervals along the top of the band, and use white running stitches to secure the bottom of the band (b).

a

b

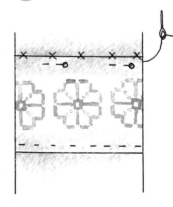

The variety of fabrics used for the tote means you can play around with combinations until you get just the right look that suits the (lucky!) recipient.

3 Appliqué the rose print fabric border below the cross stitch band and secure with pink cross stitches 2cm (¾in) apart along the top and bottom of the band. See page 111 for more on appliqué.

4 Take the grey and white spot fabric piece for the back of the bag and make sure it matches the front. With right sides together sew round the sides and along the bottom using a 6mm (¼in) seam.

5 Using the lining fabric, make a lining bag in the same way. Place the lining inside the bag, turning the top over to show on the outside and then quilt stitch along the top of the bag and the bottom edge of the lining (c).

6 Using the strap fabric strips make the straps (d). For each strap sew up one side and turn out. Press in half with the seam up the centre back. Sew the straps to the front and back of the bag about 6cm (2½in) in from the sides (e).

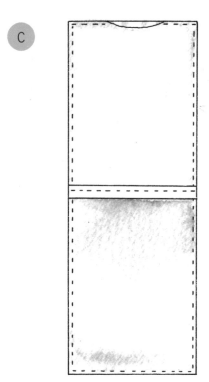

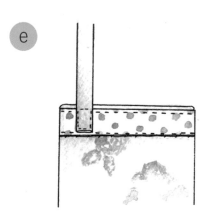

Making the buttons

1 Cross stitch a flower from the chart on to a small piece of 28-count pewter linen. Take a matching piece of pewter linen, sew around the flower shape and cut out all the way round (**f**).

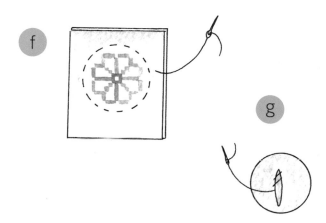

2 Make a small opening in the back, turn out, press and then stuff with polyester stuffing. Sew up the back opening (**g**). Make another button and finish by sewing them to the base of the straps on the bag front.

Need another quick gift?

• Make a bookmark by stitching a row of different coloured flowers.

• Stitch just one of the small flowers on a scrap of Aida and mount it into a key ring.

• Make a simple drawstring bag in matching grey and white spot fabric to carry smaller items in your tote.

• Make a button, add grey and white felt leaves to the back, attach a pin to give as a gift on a greetings card.

Vintage Sewing Set

This beautiful sewing set of pincushion, scissor fob and needlebook is easy to make – very vintage, very pretty and very useful at the same time. You can use up scraps of coloured linen or some companies offer sample packs of different coloured linen, which are ideal for small projects like this. Use buttons from your stash, perhaps special antique ones or visit your local craft store for the perfect match.

perfect for ...

- a child's first sewing project
- using up fabric remnants from vintage clothing
- quick gifts for a fellow sewing enthusiast

You Will Need

- 28-count linen in pale pink 10cm (4in) square

- DMC stranded cottons as in chart key

- Tapestry needle size 24–26

- Printed pink cotton for backing 10cm (4in) square

- Narrow spotted yellow ribbon

- Polyester stuffing

- Two decorative pink buttons

Finished size: 10cm (4in) square

Roses Pincushion

The rose motif used on the pincushion is timeless and works well with so many fabrics.

Sewing the motif

Find the centre of the piece of linen and, working from the centre of the chart on page 118, stitch the four rose motifs. Stitch over two threads of linen using two strands of stranded cotton for the cross stitches (a).

Sewing the pincushion

1 Take the completed stitching and place it right sides together with the backing fabric **(b)**. Sew round all sides leaving a small gap for turning **(c)**.

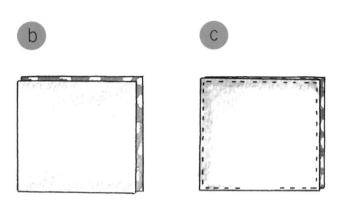

b   c

2 Trim the seams, clip the corners, turn the pincushion through to the right side and press. Stuff the pincushion with polyester stuffing and sew the gap closed.

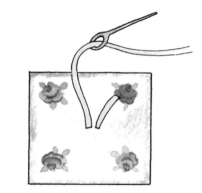

d

3 Take the ribbon and thread it through a large-eyed needle. Push the needle through the centre of the pincushion, leaving a 10cm (4in) tail of ribbon on the top **(d)**. Take the ribbon round the side of the pincushion and up through the centre again, so it looks like a parcel. Do this again for the other sides. Catch the ribbon in the centre back with a couple of stitches.

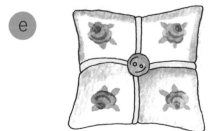

e

4 Sew a large pink button in the centre of the pincushion at the top **(e)** and a small button in the back centre to finish.

You Will Need

- Scrap of 28-count linen in pale blue
- Scrap of printed cotton fabric in blue
- DMC stranded cottons as in chart key
- Tapestry needle size 24–26
- Polyester filling
- Narrow yellow spotted ribbon
- Small pink button

Finished size: 6.5cm (2½in) square

Little Rose Scissor Fob

This sweet little scissor keeper will keep your scissors always to hand. The fob couldn't be simpler to make and you can use up precious scraps of favourite fabrics for the backing which might otherwise be too small for most projects.

Sewing the motif

Stitch the rose motif from the chart on page 118 centrally on to the piece of linen. Work over two threads of linen and use two strands of stranded cotton for the cross stitch.

Sewing the fob

1 Cut out a backing piece of blue cotton fabric and with right sides together sew round the four sides of the fob, leaving a small gap for turning. Turn right side out, trim the seams, clip the corners and press.

2 Stuff the fob with polyester stuffing and sew the gap closed with matching thread.

3 Sew a length of yellow spotted ribbon on to one corner and cover the end with a small pink button. Loop the ribbon through your scissors.

These projects are so easy to make and you can stamp your own personal style on them by your choice of embellishments.

You Will Need

- Scrap of 14-count Aida in cream

- Pieces of pink, pale green and white felt, each 12.5 x 20.5cm (5 x 8in)

- DMC stranded cottons as in chart key

- Tapestry needle size 24–26

- Fusible web (such as Bondaweb)

- One flower button and one ladybird button

- Ric-rac braid

- Matching sewing thread

Finished size: 11.5 x 9cm (4½ x 3½in)

Rosy Needlebook

Sewing will be even more of a pleasure with this oh-so-pretty needlebook to hold all your little sewing accessories.

Sewing the motif

Stitch the rose motif from the chart on page 118 centrally on to the cream Aida. Stitch over one block, using two strands of stranded cotton for the cross stitches. When the stitching is complete iron a piece of fusible web on to the back of the patch. Cut out the patch with pinking shears four holes away from the stitching.

Sewing the needlebook

1 Use pinking shears to trim the pieces of pink, pale green and white felt to 11 x 20cm (4½ x 7¾in) (a). Place the white and green felt inside the pink cover, to form pages for the needlebook (b).

2 Use matching thread to sew a line down the left-hand side of the closed needlebook 1cm (³⁄₈in) in from the fold, stitching all the felt layers together (c). Cover this stitched line with a length of pale pink ric-rac braid, sewn in place with tiny stitches and matching thread.

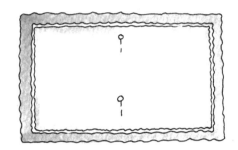

3 Fuse the embroidered patch to the front of the needlebook and add a decorative running stitch around the patch in pale pink thread.

4 Add the decorative buttons at the top and bottom of the ric-rac braid to finish.

Furry Friend Favourites

Many pet owners love giving toys to their pets and this simple bag with its dinky tag is ideal for storing them in one place, and stylish enough to look good hanging up. For dog lovers, stitch the dog toy bag shown here, and also make a dog bone toy – great for Fido to play with. If cats are more your thing, stitch the cat chart instead and make Tiddles a fish toy, perhaps filled with catnip – purrrfect!

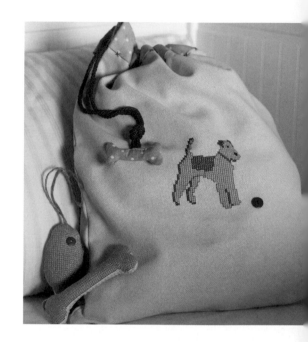

perfect for ...

• a new pet owner

• the dog or cat who has everything

• anyone who loves animal-themed gifts

You Will Need

- Pale green 18-count evenweave fabric 56 x 89cm (22 x 35in)
- Green and white spotted cotton fabric for the bag top 104 x 15cm (41 x 6in) and scraps for the bone tag
- DMC stranded cotton as in chart key
- Tapestry needle size 24–26
- Red cord about 127cm (50in) long
- Red button
- Small amount of polyester stuffing

Finished size: 53.5 x 43cm (21 x 17in)

Pet's Toy Bag

This bag is not only useful but easy to make, and the motif stitches up really quickly on the large-count evenweave fabric.

Sewing the motif

Take the evenweave fabric, fold it in half widthways and crease the fold line. Following the chart on page 119, stitch the dog (or cat) motif over two threads of evenweave in the left corner. Use three strands of cotton for the cross stitch and one strand for the backstitch. Sew on the red button near the cross stitch motif.

Sewing the bag

1 Take the strip of green spotted fabric and fold in 1cm (⅜in) on all sides. Make a small hem on the two shorter sides. Now fold the strip in half lengthways and then press.

2 Place the strip over the top of the evenweave fabric. With right side facing, measure along the length, placing pins at 2.5cm (1in) intervals. Using two strands of red stranded cotton, sew cross stitches at these intervals. Fold the strip to the inside and slipstitch in place (a).

3 Turn the fabric so that wrong sides are facing and sew up the side and bottom seams using a 6mm (¼in) seam (b). Clip the corners, turn right side out and press the bag.

a

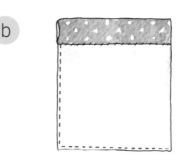

b

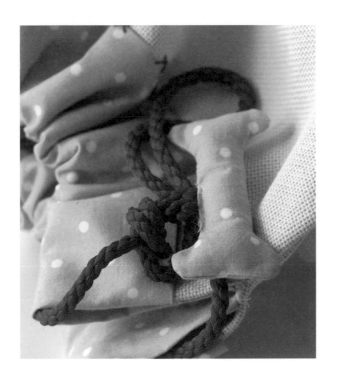

Sewing the bone tag

1 Fold a piece of green spotted fabric in half. Trace the bone template from page 122 on the wrong side of the fabric. Do not cut it out until it is stitched.

2 Sew around the bone shape, leaving an opening on one side. Cut around the shape, clip curves and turn right side out. Add polyester stuffing.

3 Thread the red cord through the channel in the top of the bag and feed the ends into the bone tag (c). Finish by stitching up the gap in the bone.

c

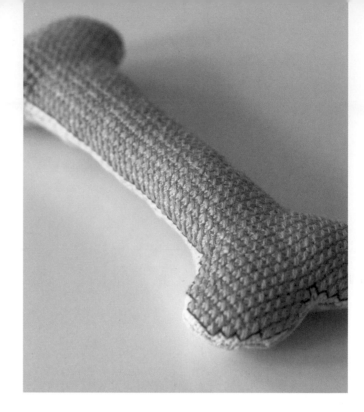

You Will Need

- Cream 18-count evenweave fabric
  11.5 x 18cm (4½ x 7in)

- DMC stranded cotton as in chart key

- Tapestry needle size 24–26

- Cream check fabric for backing
  11.5 x 18cm (4½ x 7in)

- Polyester stuffing

Finished size: 5.7 x 14cm (2¼ x 5½in)

For Fido

Throw this cute bone toy for your dog and watch him run after it – great fun for you and good exercise for him.

Sewing the motif

Stitch the bone design over two threads of the evenweave, following the chart on page 119. Use three strands of cotton for cross stitch and one strand for backstitch.

Sewing the toy

1 Press the stitching and then place right sides together with a piece of cream check cotton fabric and sew round the bone shape, following the cross stitches.

2 Make a small slit with sharp scissors in the centre back of the toy through the backing fabric. Turn the toy right side out, press and then stuff firmly with polyester filling. To finish, sew up the slit in the back neatly.

You Will Need

- Green 18-count evenweave fabric
  16.5 x 12.7cm (6½ x 5in)

- DMC stranded cotton as in chart key

- Tapestry needle size 24–26

- Green and white check cotton fabric for
  backing 16.5 x 12.7cm (6½ x 5in)

- Red button

- Polyester stuffing

- Twine for hanging loop

Finished size: 6.3 x 12cm (2½ x 4¾in)

For Tiddles

Your cat is sure to love pouncing on this fish toy
(only between naps of course…).

Sewing the motif

Stitch the fish design over two threads of the evenweave,
following the chart on page 119. Use three strands of cotton
for cross stitch and one strand for backstitch. Sew on a red
button for the eye.

Sewing the toy

1 Press the stitching and place right sides together with a
piece of cream check cotton fabric and sew round the
fish shape, following the cross stitches.

2 Make a small slit in the centre back of the toy. Turn
the toy right side out, press and then stuff firmly with
polyester filling. Sew up the slit in the back neatly. Sew the
length of twine to the fish's mouth to finish.

Bunny Cuddles

Children will love this cute toy rabbit – his sweet character shines through in his face and colourful outfit. With long arms, legs and ears, even the littlest hands can grasp him securely and enjoy his cuddly feel. Created from a basic pattern, you can dress this little bunny any way you choose. The dungarees have a cross-stitched patch and printed cotton patches stitched on with big stitches.

perfect for …

- a child's gift, and destined to become an heirloom
- wishing a little girl or boy 'get well soon'
- animal-loving children – easier to care for than a real rabbit!

You Will Need

For the rabbit

- 28-count linen in cream 0.5m (½yd)
- Scraps of blue and white spotted cotton fabric
- DMC stranded cotton for face details
- Old lipstick for the cheeks (optional)
- Polyester stuffing

For the clothes

- Scrap of white 28-count linen for patch
- DMC stranded cotton as in chart key
- Tapestry needle size 24–26
- 28-count linen in pale blue for trousers 38 x 30.5cm (15 x 12in)
- Scraps of blue felt
- Recycled stripy T-shirt
- Scraps of printed cotton for patches
- Fusible web
- Three pale blue buttons

Finished size: 39cm (15½in) tall

Sewing the rabbit

1 Fold the cream linen in half and trace the body shapes from the templates on page 123 on to the folded fabric **(a)**. Do not cut out until you have sewn around the shapes. Sew around the arms, the legs and the body **(b)**.

2 Cut out the ear shape and an ear lining from spotted cotton. Place right sides together and sew around the ear, leaving an opening at the bottom for turning. Now cut out all the shapes, turn right side out and press.

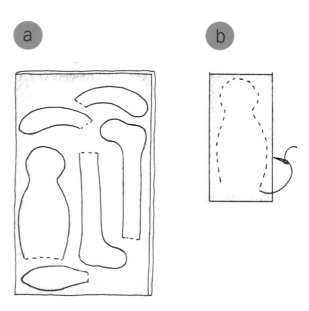

3 Using polyester filling stuff the body and then sew up along the bottom, with the seam facing front middle. Stuff the legs and sew on to the bottom of the body with the feet facing forwards **(c)**. Stuff the arms and sew to either side of the body.

4 Sew a line of running stitch along the ear opening and pull up to gather. Now sew the ears to each side of the head **(d)**.

5 To make the face, sew a nose in satin stitch, eyes in French knots and a mouth in backstitch. See page 113 for stitches. Use an old lipstick to dab on rosy colour for the cheeks. Using two strands of brown stranded cotton stitch two claws on each of the paws.

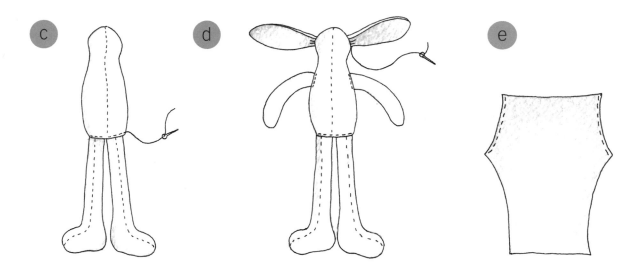

Sewing the clothes

1 Use the template on page 124 to trace the shape of the rabbit's trousers. Fold the pale blue linen in half and trace two trouser shapes on to it. Cut out the shapes and sew up the sides **(e)**. Fold the trousers with the seam up the middle and sew up the legs.

2 Sew a blue cross stitch border at the bottom of the legs, stitching over two threads with two strands of stranded cotton (**f**). Turn up a tiny hems on the trouser legs with fusible web. Make tucks along the waist band of the trousers to fit the rabbit round the middle. Appliqué two printed cotton patches to the top left leg and right leg with large stitches.

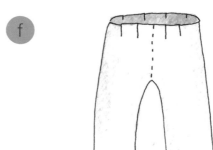

3 Cut a piece of blue felt for the bib 7 x 5cm (2¾ x 2in) and two 1 x 13cm (³⁄₈ x 5in) strips for straps. Sew the straps to the front of the bib and sew on two blue buttons (**g**). Tuck the bib behind the trousers waistband and sew with tiny running stitches. Cross the straps over at the back and sew to the trousers. Add more buttons if you wish.

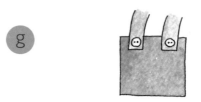

4 Using a recycled stripy T-shirt, make a T-shirt using the template on page 124. Sew it up as shown in the diagram (**h**) and then roll up the sleeves.

Sewing the motif

Stitch the cross stitch toadstool motif from the chart on page 120, working over two fabric threads and using two strands of stranded cotton for the cross stitches. Trim the fabric to about 3.8cm (1½in) square, turn over a hem all round and appliqué the patch to the left trouser leg with large red stitches. Add a blue button in the corner of the patch to finish.

Bunny Cuddles

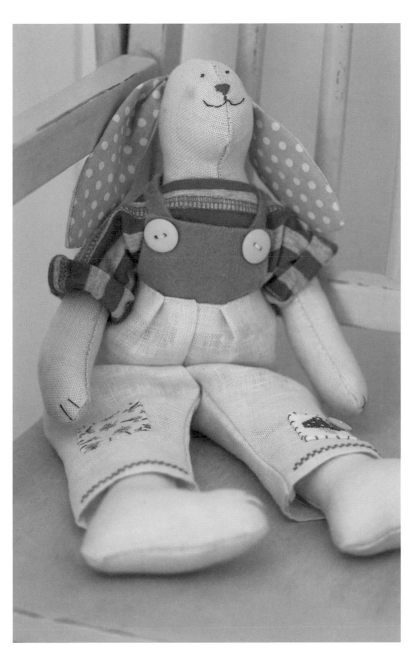
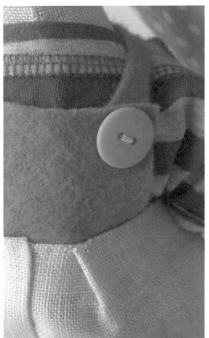
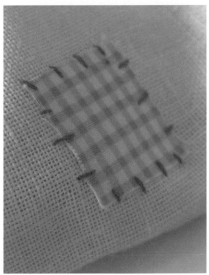

This sweet little rabbit is a gift that will be treasured for many years to come, even when his owner has grown out of all other toys.

Dolly's Cosy Quilt

Children love to tuck their toys up in bed and a sweet little quilt is a perfect gift for them. Easy to sew, it uses up fabric scraps, or you could use outgrown children's clothes. It's great fun embellishing the quilt with buttons, yo-yos, cross-stitched patches and lazy daisy flowers with tiny button centres. But remember, once you've made it the idea of making a full-size one just for you will be very, very tempting!

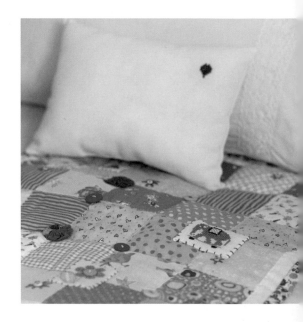

perfect for …

- little girls who adore their dolls
- bigger girls who love fabrics and embellishments
- giving as a child's wall hanging – just attach a hanger

You Will Need

- Thirty 8cm (3¼in) squares of cotton fabrics (includes seam allowances)

- White cotton fabric for border 200 x 3.8cm (78 x 1½in) approx

- Nursery print backing fabric 46 x 51cm (18 x 20in)

- Polyester wadding (batting) 46 x 51cm (18 x 20in)

- Patterned print fabric for binding 203 x 4.5cm (80 x 2½in) approx

- Scraps of white and blue 28-count linen

- DMC stranded cotton as in chart key

- Tapestry needle size 24–26

- Selection of bright buttons in small, medium and large

- Scraps of printed cottons for yo-yos

- Fusible web (such as Bondaweb)

Finished size: 42 x 48cm (16½ x 19in)

Sewing the patchwork

1 Lay out the thirty fabric squares randomly in an arrangement you like, five wide x six long. Place two of the squares right sides together and hand sew together **(a)**. Continue joining squares in this way until all the squares are joined together. Press the seams.

2 Embroider large and small lazy daisy flowers (see page 114) wherever you wish on the quilt top, sewing small buttons in the centres. Sew big buttons here and there over the quilt top, at the corners of some squares. Make four (or more) yo-yos (see page 112 for instructions) and sew them to the quilt top.

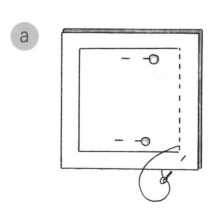

Sewing the motifs

1 Follow the chart on page 120 to stitch the toadstool motif on a scrap of white linen using two strands of stranded cotton and stitching over two threads of linen. Turn under a little hem all round and appliqué the patch to the quilt top using big red stitches. Cross stitch the elephant toy motif and apply the patch in the same way.

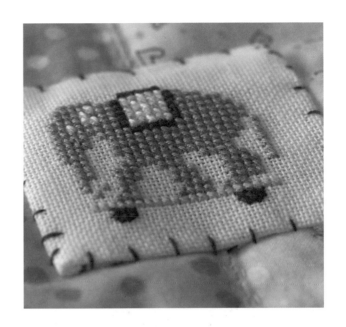

2 Stitch the flower motif from the chart and sew a button in the centre. Cut a leaf shape from printed cotton and use fusible web to appliqué it to the patch. Edge the leaf with green blanket stitch. Sew the patch to the quilt with large red stitches.

Finishing the quilt

1 Cut strips of white cotton fabric 3.8cm (1½in) wide for the borders, measuring the quilt top first. Sew the borders to the quilt, sewing on the top and bottom strips first and then the two side strips (b).

2 Place the printed backing fabric right side down on a flat surface, put the wadding (batting) on top and then add the quilt top right side up, forming a sandwich. Pin or tack (baste) through all three layers at regular intervals. Using a running stitch, quilt round the squares using white sewing thread.

b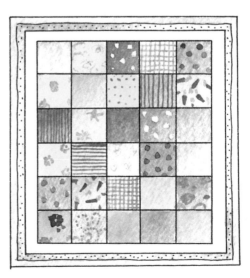

3 Using a printed cotton, bind the edges of the quilt using strips 6.3cm (2½in) wide. Assemble by placing two strips together, perpendicular to each other and stitch the strips together at a 45 degree angle. Trim the seam to 6mm (¼in) and press open. Make enough binding to go all around the quilt with about 7.5cm (3in) to spare.

4 Fold the binding in half along the length. Making sure the raw edge of the binding is aligned with the quilt edge, and beginning at one side of the quilt, pin the binding in place. At the corners, fold the binding neatly (c). Stitch the binding to the quilt, joining the two ends of the binding with a neat seam. Fold the binding over to the back of the quilt and slipstitch neatly in place.

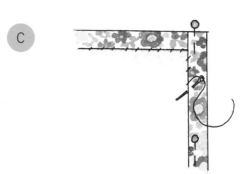

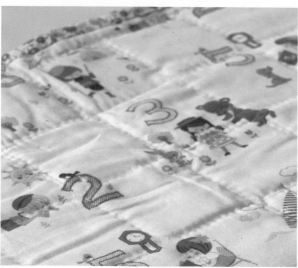

Dolly's Cosy Quilt

Children will love the little details and bright colours on this gorgeous miniature quilt. It's so easy to create that you'll want to make lots!

Festive Hearts

With their contemporary look these gorgeous fabric hearts make stylish Christmas decorations. They are fun and simple to create and are made using fresh, colourful fabrics, with felt and fabric appliqué and cross stitch motifs. You can play around with the basic idea, adding your own embellishments, such as berries, ribbons, buttons and fabrics from your own stash.

perfect for ...

- saying thank you for festive hospitality or to give to guests
- a new home – they'll become a fixture
- filling with scented pot-pourri

You will need

(for one heart)

- Printed cotton in pink and white (stripes, spots or floral) for the heart, two pieces each 18 x 10cm (7 x 4in)

- Scrap of green printed cotton fabric

- Scraps of white 28-count linen

- Tapestry needle size 24–26

- DMC stranded cotton as in chart key

- Fusible web (such as Bondaweb)

- Polyester stuffing

- Scrap of pale green felt

- Red button

- Green ribbon 24cm (9in) long

- Water-soluble or erasable marking pen

Finished size: 16.5 x 9cm (6½ x 3½in)

Sewing the motif

These instructions describe making one heart but all three hearts are made in the same way. Take a small piece of white 28-count linen and using the chart on page 121, cross stitch the motif in the centre of the linen using two strands of stranded cotton over two threads of linen. When all the cross stitching is complete, iron a piece of fusible web on to the back of the linen.

Sewing the hearts

1 Trace the heart template on page 124 on to one of the pink and white fabric pieces using a water-soluble or erasable pen.

2 Cut a small patch of green printed fabric and iron fusible web on to the back. Fuse this patch to the heart front. Now fuse the cross stitch patch in place, slightly overlapping the top corner of the green patch. Sew around the outside of the patches with two strands of red or green cotton and large stitches.

3 Take the backing piece for the heart and with right sides together sew round the heart leaving a small opening on the lower seam for turning through (a). Turn the right way out and press carefully.

4 Stuff the heart with polyester filling and sew up the opening (b). Fold the green ribbon in two and sew to the top of the heart for a hanging loop. If any marking pen is showing spray it lightly with water and blot with kitchen paper.

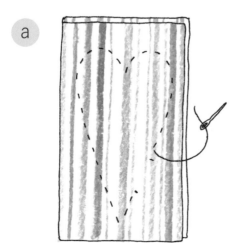

a

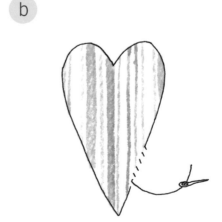

b

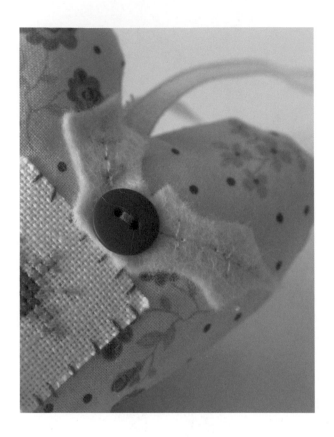

5 Take a piece of green felt and cut out two simple holly leaves, sewing leaf markings up the centre with green cotton and backstitch (c). Sew the leaf in place near the top of the heart and add a red button in the centre, sewn on with red cotton.

Need another quick gift?

- Stitch or appliqué a heart as a keepsake with a number to signify a friend's birthday or with their initials.

- These hearts make fun bag charms and oversized key rings for girls on the move.

- If you've bought a gift but want a handmade touch, pop a little fabric heart into the package – it really shows you care.

These lovely heart decorations can be hung on the Christmas tree, or on door knobs or be strung in a line on ribbon.

Christmas Stocking

The creation of a Christmas stocking is always a delight and to make a child's first stocking is a special joy. This stocking has a timeless appeal and is suitable for both children and adults. It is made in Nordic red and white style, with appliqué and quilting and a little cross stitch. The dangling decorations can be used to embellish Christmas parcels too, and you could also stitch initials or names on them.

perfect for ...

- a child's first Christmas stocking
- creating an heirloom to be cherished down the years
- using up scraps of bright Christmas fabrics

You Will Need

For the stocking

- 28-count linen in cream 6.5 x 15cm (2½ x 6in)
- DMC stranded cottons as in chart key
- Tapestry needle size 24–26
- Unbleached calico 0.5m (½yd) approx
- Small pieces of assorted red and white checked and striped cottons
- Fusible web (such as Bondaweb)
- Matching sewing thread
- 2oz wadding (batting)
- Seven white buttons

For the dangling decorations

- Scraps of 28-count linen in cream
- A few red and white seed beads
- Three tiny white buttons and three tiny red
- Polyester stuffing
- Red and white check ribbon

Finished size: 44.5 x 23cm (17½ x 9in)

Sewing the motif

Stitch the motif from the centre of the linen strip and from the centre of the chart on page 121, using two strands of stranded cotton for the cross stitch over two threads of linen.

Christmas Stocking

Sewing the stocking

1 Trace the stocking template on page 127 on to the calico, adding a 1.5cm (⅝in) seam allowance. Cut four pieces in total – one for the back, one for the front and a lining piece for each (a).

2 Cut five straight strips of red and white check fabric to form borders, each about 16.5cm (6½in) long but of variable widths. Iron fusible web on to the backs of the pieces.

3 Iron fusible web on to the back of the assorted red and white patterned fabrics. Enlarge and trace the trees, stars and moon templates from page 122 on to the web (b). Cut out the appliqué shapes.

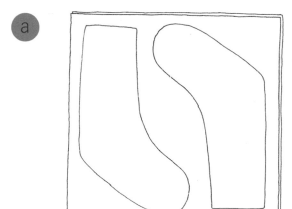

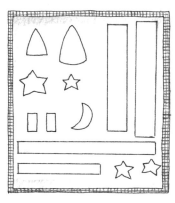

4 Arrange the appliqué pieces and the border strips on the front piece of the stocking and when you are happy with the appearance, iron them in place **(c)**. Sew around the borders and appliqués with red cotton and blanket stitch (see page 113) **(d)**.

5 Fold over the long edges of the strip of cross stitched linen and slip stitch it in place with matching thread near the top of the stocking front. Sew on the decorative buttons.

6 Place the front of the stocking and its lining piece together, and put a piece of wadding the same size between the layers, like a sandwich. Using cream thread quilt around the shapes through all three layers.

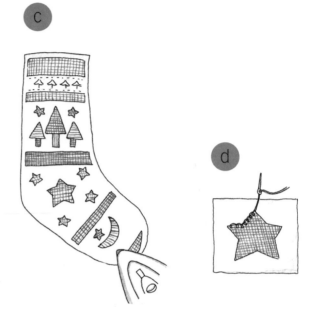

7 Take the backing piece of calico and its lining piece and put wadding in the middle as before. Using cream thread sew small star stitches randomly over the surface to hold the layers in place **(e)**.

8 Make a loop from red and white striped fabric. Place the front and back of the stocking right sides together, catching the loop in the seam near the top, and sew around the stocking. Trim the seams and clip the curves. Turn right way out and bind the top with a small strip of calico to finish.

Christmas Stocking

Sewing the dangling decorations

1 Working on scraps of 28-count cream linen, cross stitch the tree designs from the chart on page 120, using two strands of cotton for the cross stitch and working over two threads of linen. When the stitching is complete sew on the buttons and beads randomly.

2 Cut out an oblong shape 1.5cm (⅝in) away from the stitching and cut another piece of linen to match. With right sides together sew round the oblong, leaving a gap for turning.

3 Trim the seams, clip the corners and turn right side out. Stuff firmly with polyester filling and then sew up the gap. Sew the check ribbon to the top and hang from the stocking loop.

Need another quick gift?

- Sew the cross stitch on a strip of linen and make up as a bookmark.

- Make the appliquéd shapes three-dimensional and hang them from the Christmas tree.

This fabulous Christmas stocking will fit perfectly into modern interiors and can be used purely for decoration if you wish.

Bearing Gifts

This chapter has lovely gift ideas in the shape of some gorgeous little bags and a stylish cake band. The bags are stitched with Christmas motifs and use scraps of printed cottons in festive colours as binding. A matching cake band shown on page 102 completes the pretty Christmas table. The cross stitch motifs in these projects are perfect for a beginner and could also be stitched for simple cards.

perfect for . . .

- last-minute gifts
- hanging on the backs of dining rooms chairs as gifts for guests
- grouping together as a centrepiece for the Christmas table

You Will Need

- Two pieces of 28-count linen in white
  14 x 10cm (5½ x 4in) plus seam allowances
- Red and white printed fabric for binding
  3 x 32cm (1¼ x 12½in)
- Red and white striped ribbon 60cm (24in)
- DMC stranded cotton as in the key
- Tapestry needle size 24–26

Finished size: 14 x 10cm (5½ x 4in)

Star Gift Bag

This sweet little drawstring bag would be perfect to hold a precious gift, perhaps jewellery or other sparkly trinket. You could also use it in the kitchen all year long to store little cookie cutters or fill it with star anise spice for special recipes.

Sewing the bag

1 Place the two pieces of white linen together and sew up one side seam (a).

2 Withdraw five threads from the linen 4cm (1½in) down from the top, to form a row for the ribbon (b).

a

b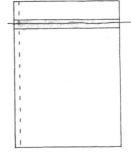

3 Sew the binding along the top edge, placing the right side of the binding together with the right side of the bag (c).

4 Stitch the star motif on to the front of the bag using the chart on page 121. Stitch over two threads of linen with two strands of stranded cotton.

5 Turn the binding over to the inside of the bag and slipstitch in place (d). Now fold the bag wrong sides together and sew round the second side of the bag and along the bottom (e).

6 Turn the bag right way out and press. Thread the ribbon through the ribbon row, pull it up and tie in a bow (f).

c

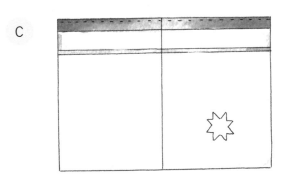

d

e

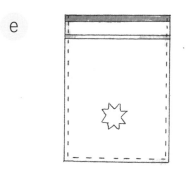

f

You Will Need

- Two pieces of 28-count linen in white 18 x 12cm (7 x 4¾in), plus seam allowances
- Red and white printed cotton for binding 3.5 x 38cm (1½ x 15in)
- Green and white spotted ribbon 60cm (24in)
- DMC stranded cottons as in chart key
- Tapestry needle size 24–26

Finished size: 16.5 x 10cm (6½ x 4in)

Tree Gift Bag

This drawstring bag is made in the same way as the Star Bag but is a little bigger. It would make a wonderful treat if filled with gold- or silver-coated sugared almonds.

Sewing the bag

1 Place the two pieces of white linen together and sew up one side seam. Withdraw five threads 4cm (1½in) down from the top, to form a row for the ribbon. Sew the binding along the top edge, placing the right side of the binding together with the right side of the bag.

2 Stitch the tree motif on to the front of the bag using the chart on page 121. Stitch over two threads of linen with two strands of stranded cotton.

3 Turn the binding over to the inside of the bag and slipstitch in place. Now fold the bag wrong sides together and sew round the second side of the bag and along the bottom. Turn the bag right way out and press. Thread the ribbon through the ribbon row, pull up and tie in a bow.

You Will Need

- 28-count linen in white 15 x 24cm (6 x 9½in)

- Red, pink and green printed cotton for binding
  3 x 27cm (1¼ x 10½in)

- Red, pink and green printed cotton for hanging
  loop 15 x 4cm (6 x 1½in)

- Bright green narrow ribbon 60cm (24in)

- DMC stranded cotton as in chart key

- Tapestry needle size 24–26

Finished size: 14 x 10cm (5½ x 4in)

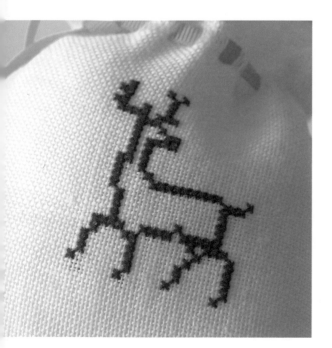

Reindeer Gift Bag

Children would have fun filling this reindeer motif
bag with treats for Santa and Rudolph on Christmas
Eve. The bag has a hanging loop on the back so
could be hung from the mantelpiece or tree.

Sewing the bag

1 Start by sewing the binding along the top edge of the
linen by placing the right side of the binding together
with the right side of the linen (a).

a

2 Withdraw four threads for the ribbon row 4cm (1½in) from the top of the bag. Now stitch the reindeer motif on to the front of the bag using the chart on page 121. Stitch over two threads of linen with two strands of stranded cotton (b).

b

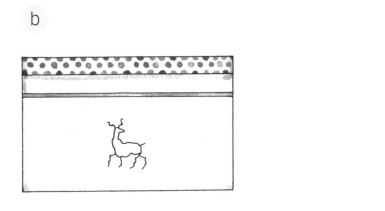

4 Make the loop for the bag by folding the strip of printed cotton fabric in half and sewing down the long edge. Turn through to the right side and press, with the seam in the middle of the back (e).

e

3 Fold the linen in half, right sides together, sew up the side seam and press (c). Position the seam at the middle of the back of the bag, sew along the bottom seam (d), turn right side out and press.

5 Turn under the ends of the loop and slipstitch to the middle of the back of the bag 2.5cm (1in) down from the top (f). Sew the other end of the loop inside the bag at the front, to correspond with the back piece (g).

c   d   f   g

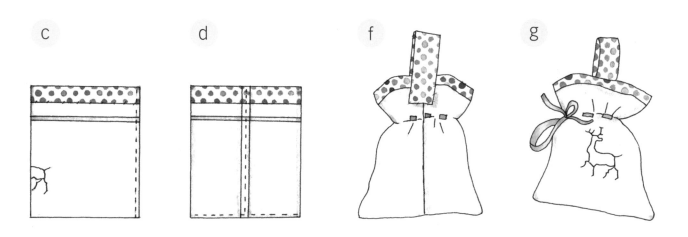

Sweet little bags are perfect to give on their own or filled with seasonally scented pot-pourri or sweet treats.

You Will Need

- Strip of 14-count white Aida 7.5cm (3in) deep x length to fit around your cake

- Two strips of red and white printed cotton for binding, 3cm (1¼in) wide x length of the Aida strip

- DMC stranded cottons as in the key

- Tapestry needle size 24–26

- Velcro dots

Finished size: 3in (7.6cm) wide x length of your choice to fit around cake

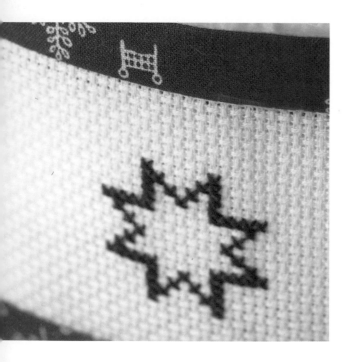

Festive Cake Band

This cake band can be made in any length to fit your cake and the colour of the stitching and binding changed to whatever you like – perhaps a festive green or frosty blue.

Sewing the band

1 Place one strip of binding fabric right sides together with the Aida strip and sew them together along the length. Turn the binding over, fold under a small hem and sew to the Aida along the back. Repeat this for the bottom length of binding.

2 Fold the bound Aida strip in half to find the centre and begin stitching here over one Aida block following the poinsettia and star chart on page 121. Use two strands of stranded cotton for the cross stitches. Count carefully between each motif to position them correctly.

3 When the stitching is complete, press your work and add Velcro dots to fasten the band around the cake.

You'll look forward to making your Christmas cake every year with this stylish cake band to decorate it with.

Mr and Mrs Gingerbread

These cute cookie-shaped toys make lovely decorations for the kitchen at any time of year. You could make Mr and Mrs Gingerbread, as shown here, or make a whole family and decorate each one in a slightly different way by using a variety of ribbons and other embellishments. You could also make padded gingerbread hearts and stars from the same linen to match the gingerbread family.

perfect for ...

- gifts for children, perhaps with sweets attached
- the cake and cookie fanatic
- those who love handmade toys

You Will Need

- 28-count linen in ginger brown for the body
  21.5 x 35.5cm (8½ x 14in)

- DMC stranded cottons as in chart key

- Tapestry needle size 24–26

- Polyester toy stuffing

- White acrylic paint

- Two white buttons

- Red and white check ribbon and
  narrow red ribbon

- Small bundle of cinnamon sticks (optional)

Finished size: 19.5 x 14.5cm (7¾ x 5¾in)

Sewing Mr Gingerbread

1 Fold the linen in half and trace the template of the body shape from page 125 on to it **(a)**. Cross stitch a tiny heart on the front using the chart on page 120. Cross stitch over two threads of linen using two strands of stranded cotton. Do not cut out the shape yet. Sew round the shape **(b)** and then cut it out and clip the curves. Cut a slit in the centre of the back for turning through.

 a

 b

2 Turn right side out, press and then stuff with polyester stuffing and sew up the gap (c).

3 Create the face using French knots and black stranded cotton for the eyes, white cotton and backstitch for the mouth. Brush on a little white acrylic paint for the cheeks and dot of white paint for the nose.

4 Using red stranded cotton, sew on the two white buttons on the front.

5 Tie the red and white check ribbon around his neck in a bow. Tie the cinnamon sticks in a bundle with narrow red ribbon (d) and tie to the left hand.

Need another quick gift?

- Create a whole range of gingerbread toys in different sizes for children to play with.

- Make gingerbread cookies, put in a cellophane bag tied with ribbon and place in a box with a gingerbread toy.

You Will Need

- 28-count linen in ginger brown for the body
  35.5 x 21.5cm (14 x 8½in)

- 28-count linen in white for the apron
  35.5 x 6.5cm (14 x 2½in)

- DMC stranded cottons as in chart key

- Tapestry needle size 24–26

- Polyester toy stuffing

- White acrylic paint

- Two red heart buttons

- Narrow white ribbon

- Tiny white bow

- Doll's cookie cutter (optional)

Finished size: 19.5 x 14.5cm (7¾ x 5¾in)

Sewing Mrs Gingerbread

1 Fold the linen in half and trace the template of the body shape from page 125 on to it. Do not cut out the shape until you have sewn round it. Sew round the shape, then cut it out and clip the curves. Cut a slit in the centre of the back for turning.

2 Turn right side out, press and then stuff with polyester stuffing and sew up the gap.

3 Create the face using French knots and black stranded cotton for the eyes, white cotton and backstitch for the mouth. Brush on a little white acrylic paint for the cheeks and dot on white paint for the nose.

Sewing the pinafore dress

1 Make a pinafore dress by cutting a 28 x 6cm (11 x 2½in) piece of white linen for the skirt. Sew a seam up the back and hem the bottom by turning up and stitching with red running stitch. Sew a red cross stitch heart from the chart on page 120, working over two threads of linen with two strands of stranded cotton (a).

2 To make the top of the dress cut a piece of linen 6.5 x 6.5cm (2½ x 2½in), turn in three sides, press and then catch down with white running stitch (b).

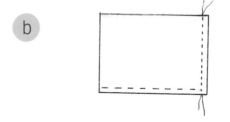

3 Place the top behind the skirt and fit the skirt to the toy by making tucks all round the top. Sew the pinafore top to the skirt. Make straps using thin white ribbon and sew to the front of the pinafore in the top right and left corners. Cross the ribbons at the back and sew them to the skirt. Sew red buttons to the pinafore top with white thread (c).

4 Sew the tiny white bow to the top of her head. To finish, sew on the cookie cutter to the right hand using matching thread.

Materials and Techniques

This section will be useful to beginners as it contains information on the materials and equipment you will need and the basic techniques needed to work the projects in the book.

Materials

Fabrics
Most of the projects are sewn with lovely printed cottons in fresh and contemporary colours and patterns. When cutting fabric add extra for seam allowances, usually 6mm–1.3cm (¼–½in) all round. Some projects use felt, which doesn't require a seam as it does not fray.

The cross stitch motifs have been worked on a blockweave fabric called Aida and on evenweave or linen fabrics. If working on Aida, stitch over one block; if working on evenweave stitch over two fabric threads.

Threads
You will need ordinary sewing thread for the projects, in colours to match your fabrics. The cross stitch motifs have been stitched with DMC stranded embroidery cotton (floss), which is available as six-stranded skeins that can be split into separate strands. The project instructions tell you how many strands to use.

Needles
Standard hand sewing and machine sewing needles will be needed to create the projects. For the cross stitch use tapestry needles, which have a rounded point and do not snag fabric. Glass seed beads are used on the Christmas Stocking and you will need a thinner beading needle to attach these.

Fabric Markers
You will need to be able to mark designs and shapes on fabric for some projects and there are many types of markers available for this. It is best to use a removable type and this may be an air-erasable type, which fades after a period of time; a water-soluble type, which can be removed with a light spray of water; or a simple chalk marker. Always test a marker on scrap fabric first.

Wadding (batting)
Wadding is used for padding and to give an attractive puffy look when quilted. There are various types of wadding available, including cotton and polyester. Choose a thin wadding that is easily sewn through for the projects in this book.

Embellishments
Various embellishments have been used on the projects, including buttons, beads, ribbons and braids. Your local craft store should have a good selection and see Suppliers on page 128 for useful addresses.

Techniques

Preparing Fabrics

Spending a little time preparing your fabric before stitching will save time and trouble in the long run.

•   Before beginning to stitch it is a good idea to neaten the fabric edges. Using pinking shears will help prevent edges from fraying.

•   If you think a fabric may not be colourfast then wash, dry and iron it before use.

•   Before stitching cross stitch on an embroidery fabric, check the finished design size given with each chart and make sure that your fabric is larger than this to allow for making up.

•   When cross stitching find the centre of the fabric and work from here outwards, to ensure the motif will fit on the fabric.

Using Templates

Templates are provided for the projects (see pages 122–126). Follow the instructions on page 122.

Using Interfacing and Fusible Web

Iron-on interfacing has a glue web on one side that melts under the heat of an iron, so it can be fused to fabrics to stiffen and stabilize them and allow the edges to be cut without fraying. Cut the interfacing to size and fuse it to the back of the fabric with a medium-hot iron. If ironing on to cross stitch embroidery then place the embroidery face down into some thick towels.

Fusible webbing is a very useful product with a glue web on both sides, which allows you to fuse one fabric to another. Using this product will allow you to fuse your cross stitch embroidery to all sorts of ready-made items. Use a medium-hot iron and refer to the manufacturer's instructions.

Fusible Web Appliqué

Appliqué is a technique where one fabric is attached to another, and the top fabric is usually cut to a pattern or shape. Many of the projects use appliqué and it's really easy especially if you use fusible web, which has a glue web on both sides.

Draw the design or shape on the paper backing of the fusible web and roughly cut out the shape. Place your appliqué fabric right side down and place the fusible web shape glue side down on top of the fabric. Iron with a medium iron to fuse it to the fabric. Cut out the shape following your drawn line. Peel off the backing paper and place the patch right side up on the right side of the background fabric and fuse into place. The edges of the appliqué can be further secured with various stitches, including blanket stitch, large straight stitches, running stitch or machine satin stitch.

Making a Quilt 'Sandwich'

When a project is quilted, a quilt 'sandwich' is often created to give that nice padded look. Simply place your backing fabric right side down on a flat surface, place the piece of wadding on top and then the top fabric or patchwork right side up on top of this. Secure these three layers with safety pins or sewing pins, ready for quilting. Use a running stitch to quilt through the three layers.

Attaching Beads

Attach beads using a beading needle or very fine 'sharp' needle. Use thread that matches the bead colour and secure with either a half cross stitch or a full cross stitch.

Making a Yo-yo

Yo-yos make attractive embellishments and can be used on all sorts of projects, especially if you want a three-dimensional look.

   To make a yo-yo start with a circle of fabric twice the size that you want the finished yo-yo to be (a). Fold the edges over all round by 6mm (¼in) and use strong sewing thread to make a running stitch all round this folded edge (b). Pull the thread up and gather the fabric so only a small gap remains. Secure the thread and press the yo-yo (c). The yo-yo can then be attached to a fabric base, gathered side up, with slipstitches. You could add a button or bead or some decorative stitches, such as French knots, in the centre if you wish.

 a

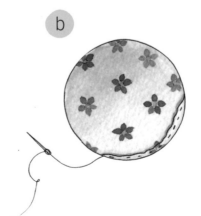 b

 c

The Stitches

Starting and Finishing

Starting and finishing cross stitch embroidery correctly will create the neatest effect and avoid bumps and threads trailing across the back of work.

Thread your needle and make a knot at the end. Take the needle and thread through from the front of the fabric to the back and come up again about 2.5cm (1in) away from the knot. Now either start cross stitching and work towards the knot, cutting it off when the threads are anchored, or thread the end into your needle and finish the thread off under some completed stitches.

To finish off thread, pass the needle through several nearby stitches on the wrong side of the work and then cut the thread off close to the fabric.

~kstitch

~h is shown on charts by a coloured line. It ~ked on its own for lettering, on top of for detail and as an outline arou~ ~nition. It is normally w~

Blanket Stitch

This stitch is used decoratively to edge appliqué motifs and can be spaced according to your preference. When very tightly spaced it is called buttonhole stitch.

To work blanket stitch, bring the needle and thread out at 1 in the diagram below, insert it at 2 and then bring out at 3. Keeping the thread under the needle, pull the thread so that it lies snugly against the fabric without distortion. Continue in the same way, following the outline of the motif you are edging.

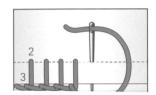

Fig 2 Working blanket stitch

~e embroidered motifs.
~own on the charts by a
~d over two threads of
~of Aida.
~ stages: a diagonal
~(or one block), then a
~over the first stitch in
~cross (see diagrams).
~ches in two journeys,
~tches in one
~posite direction
~o complete each
~ld lie in the same

A single cross
~ evenweave

Three-quarter Cross Stitch

This is a part stitch or fractional stitch used to add detail to a design and create curves. It is shown on charts by a coloured triangle within a square.

To work three-quarter cross stitch, work a half cross stitch, then add a quarter stitch in the opposite direction, bringing the needle down in the centre of the half cross stitch already worked (see diagram).

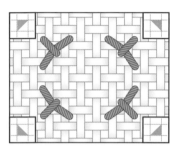

Fig 4 *Working three-quarter cross stitch*

French Knot

This is a useful little stitch and may be used in addition to cross stitch to add texture and emphasis. In this book they are usually worked with two strands of thread wound once around the needle, and are shown on the charts by a small coloured circle.

To work a French knot, bring the needle up to the right side of the fabric, hold the thread down with your left thumb (if right-handed) and wind the thread around the needle twice (see diagram below). Still holding the thread taut put the needle through to the back of the work, one thread or part of a block away from the entry point. If you want bigger knots, add more strands of thread to the needle.

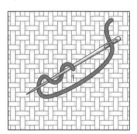

Fig 5 *Working a French knot*

Lazy Daisy Stitch

This stitch is used on Dolly's Cosy Quilt to add decorative detail. It is very easy to work, just make a loop and anchor it with a little stitch, as shown in the diagram below.

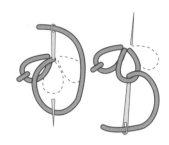

Fig 6 *Working lazy daisy stitch*

Running Stitch

A long running stitch can be used to gather fabrics, while a shorter running stitch is used for quilting. You don't have to work small stitches when quilting – find the length that suits you.

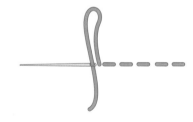

Fig 7 *Working running stitch or quilting stitch*

Satin Stitch

Satin stitch is normally used as a filling stitch to give blocks of thread colour. It is used for facial details in the delightful Bunny Cuddles toy.

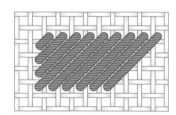

Fig 8 *Working satin stitch*

The Charts

The cross stitch charts required for the projects are all given in this section, predominantly in the book order. Some projects only feature part of the cross stitch design, so look at the project photographs before you begin stitching.

 Full cross stitches are shown by coloured squares, sometimes with a symbol to distinguish shades.

 Three-quarter cross stitches are shown by coloured triangles, sometimes with a symbol to distinguish shades.

— Backstitches are shown by thick coloured lines.

● French knots are shown by a coloured circle.

 Each complete chart or motif has arrows at the side to show the centre point, which you could mark with a pen.

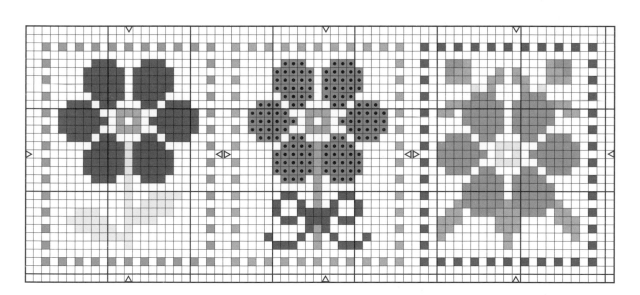

Breakfast Set
DMC stranded cotton
Cross stitch (2 strands)

▨ 165	▨ 3607	▨ 3836
▨ 907	● 3716	

Cafetière
Stitch flowerhead only
Stitch count:
15h x 17w

Design size:
1 x 1¼in (2.5 x 3cm)

Egg Cosy
Stitch count:
27h x 21w each

Design size:
2 x 1½in (5 x 3.8cm)

Napkin
Stitch flowerhead only
Stitch count:
15h x 17w

Design size:
1 x 1¼in (2.5 x 3cm)

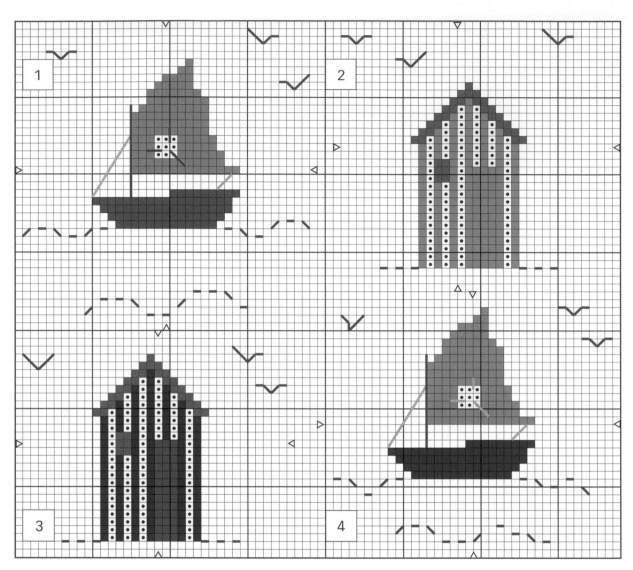

Laundry Bag and Bunting
DMC stranded cotton
Cross stitch (2 strands)

- 317
- 349
- 996
- 3608
- 3807
- • blanc

Backstitch (1 strand)
— 317
— 318

Bunting
Stitch counts:
1) 37h x 37w
2) 31h x 30w
3) 25h x 35w
4) 30h x 36w

Design sizes:
1) 2¾ x 2¾in (6.7 x 6.7cm)
2) 2¼ x 2¼in (5.5 x 5.5cm)
3) 1¾ x 2½in (4.5 x 6.3cm)
4) 2¼ x 2½in (5.5 x 6.5cm)

Laundry Bag
Stitch count: 25h x 24w

Design size:
1¾ x 1¾in (4.5 x 4.5cm)

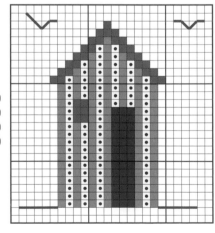

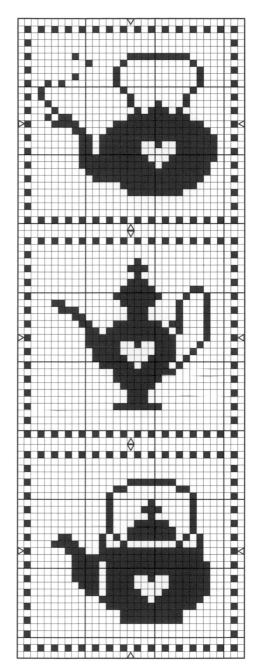

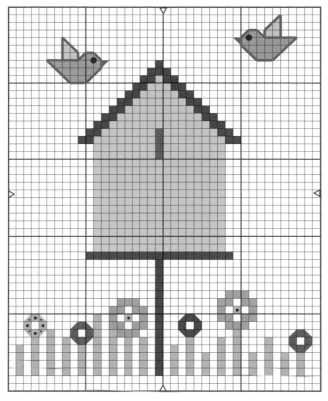

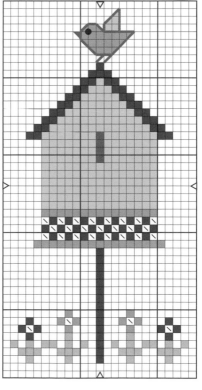

Bistro Wall Hanging
DMC stranded cotton
Cross stitch (2 strands)

■ 601

Stitch count: (each motif)
29h x 31w

Design size:
2 x 2¼in (5.2 x 5.6cm)

Retro Apron and Recipe Book
DMC stranded cotton
Cross stitch (2 strands)

▨ 704		▨ 3799
▨ 793		▨ 3849
▨ 3328		• 3855
▨ 3354		╲ blanc
▨ 3761		

Backstitch (1 strand)
—— 3799

French knots (2 strands)
● 3799

Retro Apron
Stitch count: 47h x 38w

Design size:
3½ x 2¾in (8.5 x 7cm)

Recipe Book
Stitch count: 46h x 23w

Design size:
3¼ x 1¾in (8.3 x 4.2cm)

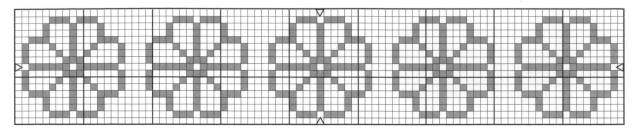

Mix 'n' Match Tote
DMC stranded cotton
Cross stitch (2 strands)

▨ 818

Stitch count:
15h x 87w

Design size:
1 x 61/4in (2.5 x 15.8cm)

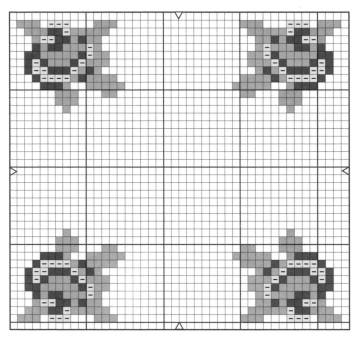

Roses Pincushion, Rosy Needlebook and Little Rose Scissor Fob
DMC stranded cotton
Cross stitch (2 strands)

▨ 704

− 744

▨ 3328

▨ 3716

Roses Pincushion
Stitch count:
39h x 42w

Design size:
2¾ x 3in
(7 x 7.5cm)

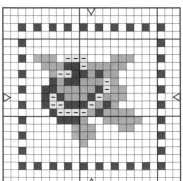

Rosy Needlebook
Stitch count:
19h x 19w

Design size:
1¼ x 1¼in
(3.4 x 3.4cm)

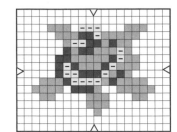

Little Rose Scissor Fob
Stitch count: 12h x 16w

Design size:
¾ x 1¼in (2.2 x 3cm)

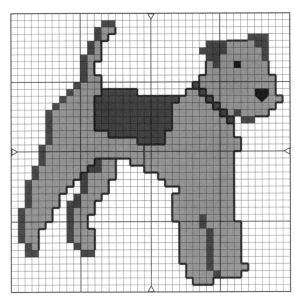

Dog Toy Bag
DMC stranded cotton
Cross stitch (3 strands)

■	310	
■	433	Backstitch (1 strand)
■	437	▬ 433
■	3328	▬ 3328

Dog Toy Bag
Stitch count: 38h x 38w

Design size: 4¼ x 4¼in
(10.7 x 10.7cm)

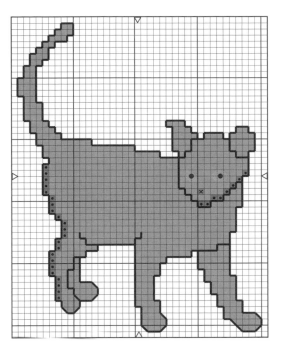

Cat Toy Bag
DMC stranded cotton
Cross stitch (3 strands)

✕	352	■	597
■	437	●	832

Backstitch (1 strand)
▬ 433

French knots
● 310

Cat Toy Bag
Stitch count: 50h x 39w

Design size: 5½ x 4½in
(14 x 11cm)

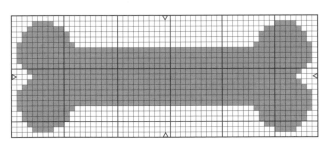

Bone Toy
DMC stranded
cotton
Cross stitch
(3 strands)

■ 437

Stitch count: 21h x 56w

Design size: 2½ x 6¼in
(6 x 15.8cm)

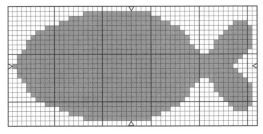

Fish Toy
DMC stranded cotton
Cross stitch (3 strands)

■ 597

Stitch count: 23h x 50w

Design size: 2½ x 5½in
(6.5 x 14cm)

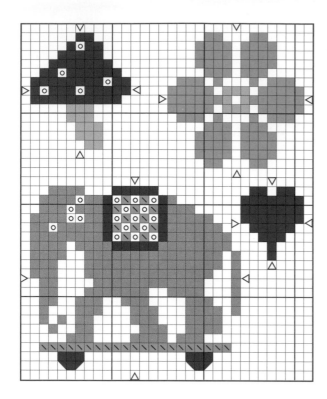

Bunny Cuddles and Dolly's Cosy Quilt
DMC stranded cotton
Cross stitch (2 strands)

■	349	▨	760
▨	519	╲	3845
▨	642	○	blanc
▨	704		

Rabbit and Quilt
Stitch counts:
Toadstool: 13h x 11w
Flower: 15h x 15w
Elephant: 20h x 23w
Heart: 8h x 7w

Design sizes:
Toadstool: 1 x ¾in (2.5 x 2cm)
Flower: 1 x 1in (2.5 x 2.5cm)
Elephant: 1½ x 1¾in (3.7 x 4.2cm)
Heart: ½ x ½in (1.3 x 1.3cm)

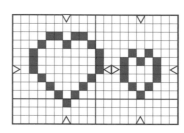

Gingerbread Couple
DMC stranded cotton
Cross stitch (2 strands)

■ 3328

Stitch counts:
Large 9h x 9w
Small 6h x 5w

Design sizes:
Large ¾ x ¾in (2 x 2cm)
Small ½ x ¼in (1.3 x 0.6cm)

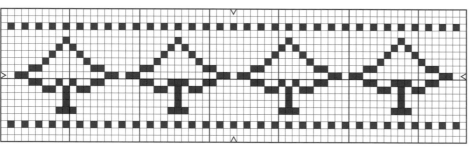

Christmas Stocking and Dangling Decorations
DMC stranded cotton
Cross stitch (2 strands)

■ 601

Christmas Stocking
Stitch count: 15h x 65w

Design size: 1 x 4¾in (2.5 x 11.8cm)

Dangling Decorations
Stitch count: 23h x 17w each

Design size: 1¾ x 1¼in (4.2 x 3cm)

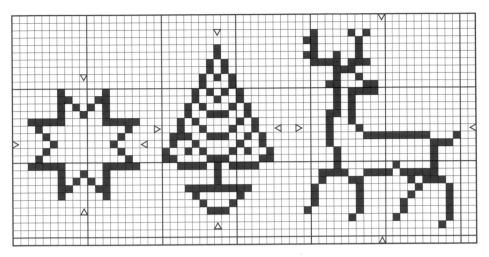

Gift Bags
DMC stranded cotton
Cross stitch (2 strands)

■ 321

Stitch counts:
Star: 13h x 11w
Tree: 15h x 15w
Reindeer: 20h x 23w

Design sizes:
Star: 1 x ¾in (2.5 x 2cm)
Tree: 1 x 1in (2.5 x 2.5cm)
Reindeer: 1½ x 1¾in (3.7 x 4.2cm)

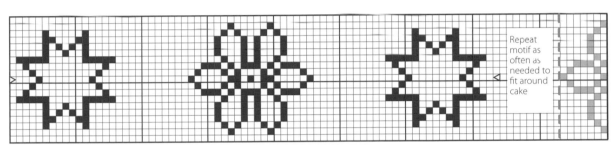

Repeat motif as often as needed to fit around cake

Cake Band
DMC stranded cotton
Cross stitch (2 strands)

■ 321

Stitch count: 17h x length to fit cake

Design size: 1¼in (3cm) x length to fit cake

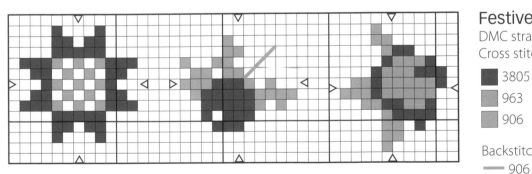

Festive Hearts
DMC stranded cotton
Cross stitch (2 strands)

■ 3805
■ 963
■ 906

Backstitch (2 strands)
— 906

Stitch count: 11h x 11w

Design size:
¾ x ¾in (2 x 2cm)

Stitch count: 9h x 11w

Design size:
½ x ¾in (1.6 x 2cm)

Stitch count: 12h x 10w

Design size:
¾ x ¾in (2.2 x 2cm)

The Templates

The project templates are given in this section and all are given at actual size . To use a template trace the outline on to thin card or thick paper and cut out the shape. Place the shape on your fabric and draw around it. If no seam allowance is needed cut out the shape on the line. If the fabric needs a seam allowance then cut out the shape further out, usually ¼in–½in (6mm–1.3cm) all round.

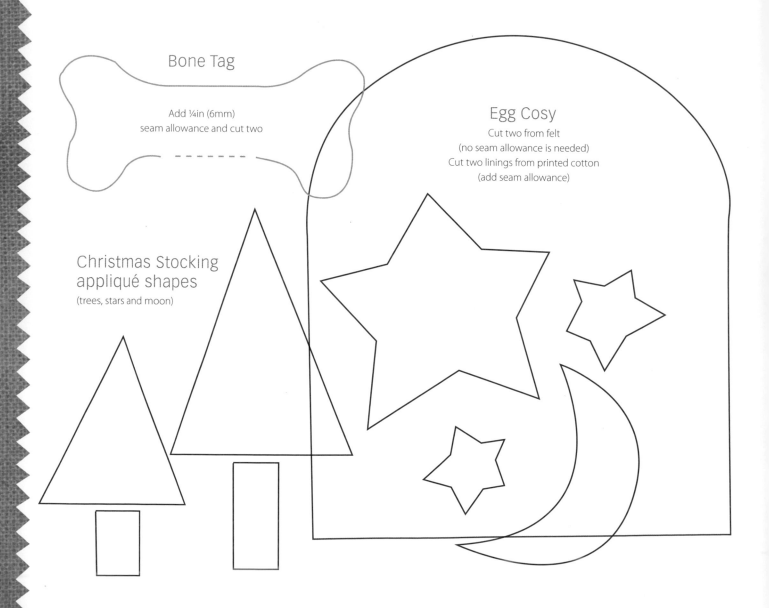

Bone Tag

Add ¼in (6mm)
seam allowance and cut two

Egg Cosy
Cut two from felt
(no seam allowance is needed)
Cut two linings from printed cotton
(add seam allowance)

Christmas Stocking
appliqué shapes
(trees, stars and moon)

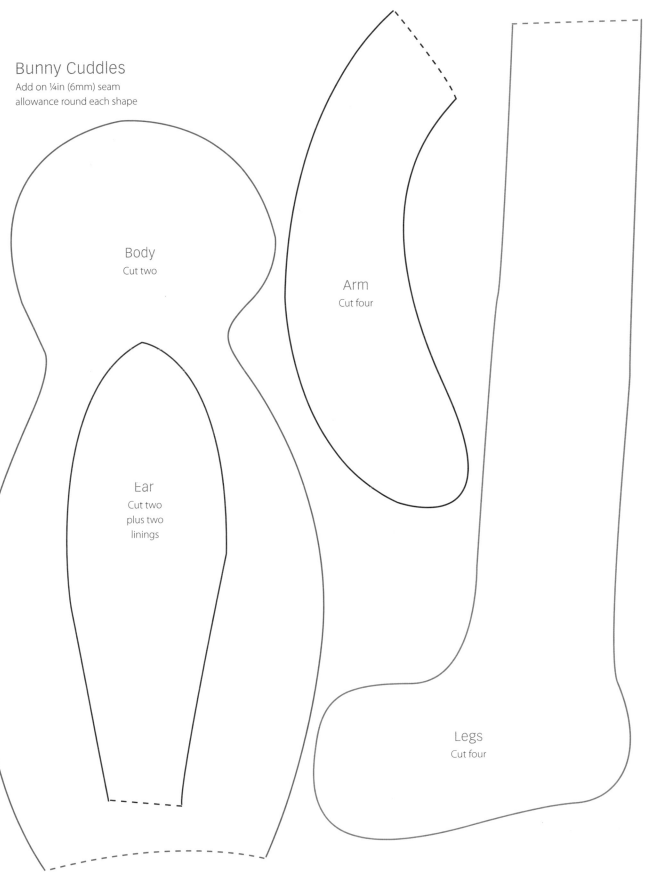

Bunny Cuddles

Add on ¼in (6mm) seam
allowance round each shape

Body
Cut two

Ear
Cut two
plus two
linings

Arm
Cut four

Legs
Cut four

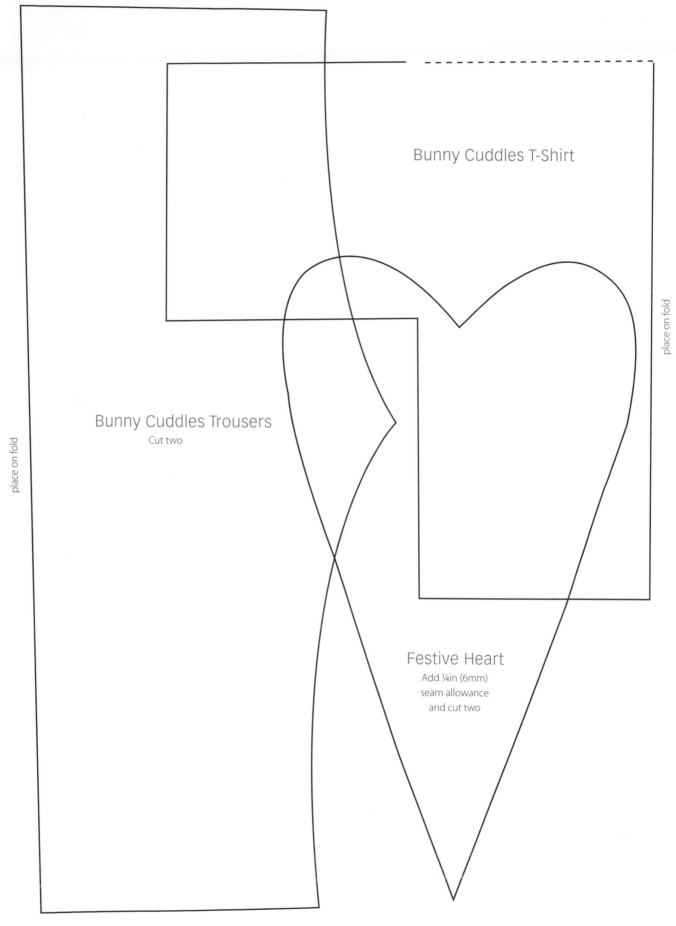

Bunny Cuddles T-Shirt

place on fold

place on fold

Bunny Cuddles Trousers

Cut two

Festive Heart
Add ¼in (6mm)
seam allowance
and cut two

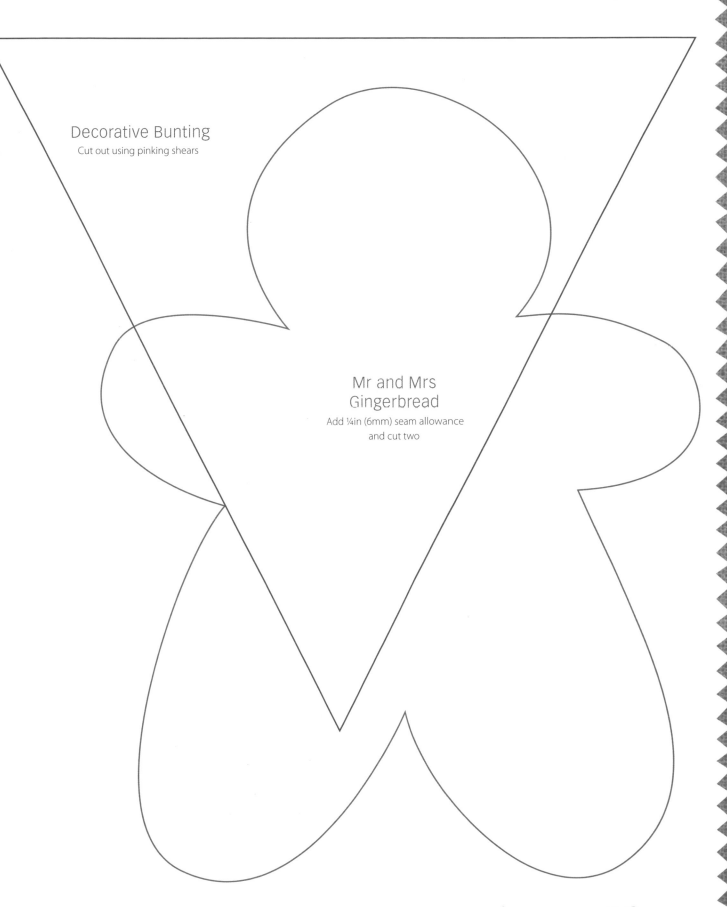

Decorative Bunting
Cut out using pinking shears

Mr and Mrs Gingerbread
Add ¼in (6mm) seam allowance and cut two

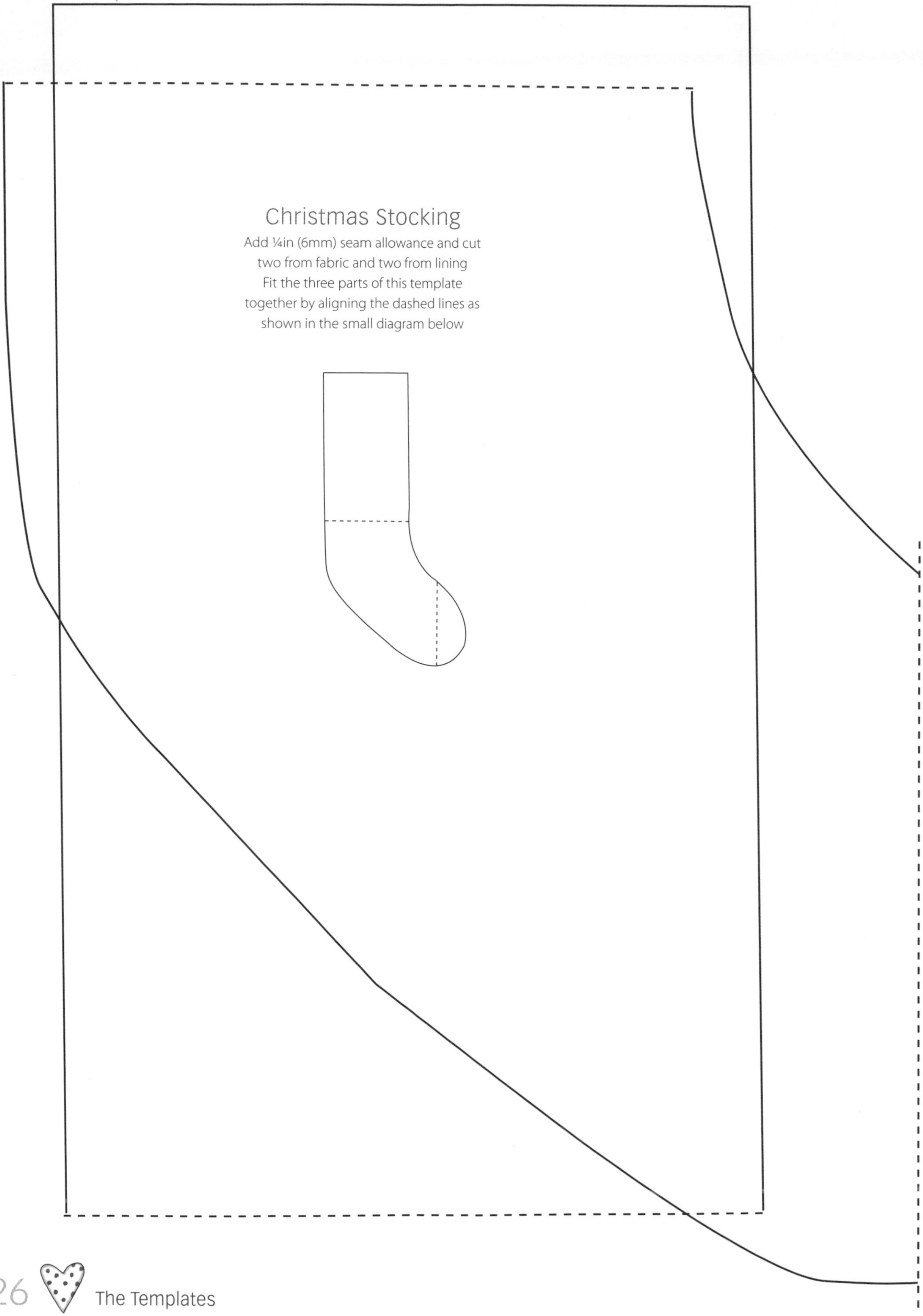

Christmas Stocking

Add ¼in (6mm) seam allowance and cut
two from fabric and two from lining
Fit the three parts of this template
together by aligning the dashed lines as
shown in the small diagram below

Acknowledgments

Thank you to the whole team at David & Charles. Thank you especially to Jennifer Fox-Proverbs for believing in my stitch and craft designs and commissioning this book, and for bringing it all together with such creative flair. Thank you to my editor Lin Clements, as always, for her skill, patience and amazing attention to detail when editing the text and the charts. Thanks to Sian Irvine and Joe Giacomet for the delightful photography and to Victoria Marks for the stunning book design. Finally, a big thank you to my wonderful husband David and my lovely family for all their encouragement and support.

About the Author

Helen Philipps studied printed textiles and embroidery at Manchester Metropolitan University and then taught drawing and design before becoming a freelance designer. After working in the greetings card industry, Helen's love of needlecraft led her to create original designs for stitching magazines and later for books. Her work features regularly in *Crafts Beautiful, Let's Make Cards, Let's Get Crafting, Cross Stitcher* and *Cross Stitch Collection*. This is Helen's seventh book for David & Charles following on from *Cross Stitch Keepsakes* in 2008.

Suppliers

UK

Debbie Cripps
8 Christchurch Street West,
Frome, Somerset BA11 1EQ
Tel: 01373 454448
www.debbiecripps.co.uk
*For aperture boxes, beads, buttons,
charms and many other supplies*

DMC Creative World Limited
1st Floor Compass Building,
Feldspar Close, Warrens Park,
Enderby, Leicester, LE19 4SD
Tel: 0116 2754000
www.dmccreative.co.uk
www.dmc.com
For DMC fabrics and threads

Sew and So
Stroud House, Russell Street,
Stroud, Glos GL5 3AN
Tel: 01453 889988
www.sewandso.co.uk
*For Just Another Button Company
buttons, coloured linen and threads*

US

Charles Craft Inc.
The DMC Corporation, 10 Basin
Drive, Suite 130, Kearny, NJ 07032,
USA
Tel: 973 589 0606
www.charlescraft.com
For fabrics and threads for cross stitch

Joann Stores, Inc
5555 Darrow Road, Hudson,
OH 44236, USA
Tel: 1 888 739 4120
www.joann.com
*For general sewing and quilting
supplies (mail order and shops
across US)*

www.superbuzzy.com
For fabrics and sewing accessories

www.reprodepotfabrics.com
For fabrics and sewing accessories

Index

appliqué 46, 48–50, 70, 75, 80, 89–90, 111, 122
aprons 34–9, 117

backstitch 113
bags
    gift 94–101, 121
    laundry 16–21
    for pets 60–3, 119, 122
    tote 46–51, 118
beach hut motifs 18, 25, 116
beads 112
bird house motifs 36, 42, 117
blanket stitch 113
boat motifs 25, 116
books, recipe 40–3, 117
breakfast sets 8–15, 115
bunting 22–7, 116, 125

cafetière covers 10–12, 115
cake bands 94–5, 102–3, 121
clothing, toy 66, 69–70, 109, 124
cross stitch 113–21

dolls 72–7, 104–9, 120, 125

egg cosies 14–15, 115, 122
elephant toy motif 75, 120

fabrics 110, 111
fish designs 65, 119
flower designs 11–15, 36, 46–52, 56, 58,
    74–5, 102, 115, 118, 120–1
French knots 114
fusible web 111

heart designs 80–5, 106, 109, 120–1, 124

iron-on interfacing 111

kettle motifs 30, 117

lazy daisy stitches 114
leaves 75, 84

markers 110
materials 110
moon designs 89–90, 122

napkins 13, 115
needlebooks 52, 58–9, 118
needles 110

patchwork 72–7
pet projects 60–5, 119, 122
pincushions 52, 54, 118
pockets 31–2, 34, 38

poinsettia motif 102, 121

quilts 72–7, 112, 120

rabbits, toy 66–71, 120, 123–4
reindeer designs 99–100, 121
rose motifs 52, 56, 58, 118, 121
running stitches 114

satin stitches 114
scissor fobs 52, 56–7, 118
seam allowances 110
sewing sets 52–9
star designs 82, 89–90, 96–7, 102, 121–2
stitches 113–14
stockings, Christmas 86–93, 120, 126–7

techniques 111–14
templates 111, 122–7
threads 110
toadstool motifs 70, 75, 120
toys 64–77, 104–9, 119–20, 122–4, 125
tree designs 88–90, 93, 98, 120–2

wadding (batting) 110
wall hangings 28–33, 117

yo-yos 12–15, 74, 112